D1343858

THE Z TO Z OF GREAT BRITAIN

DIXE WILLS

ICON BOOKS

Originally published in the UK in 2005
by Icon Books Ltd

Reprinted 2005

This edition published in the UK in 2006 by
Icon Books Ltd, The Old Dairy,
Brook Road, Thriplow, Cambridge SG8 7RG
email: info@iconbooks.co.uk
www.iconbooks.co.uk

Sold in the UK, Europe, South Africa and Asia
by Faber & Faber Ltd, 3 Queen Square, London WC1N 3AU
or their agents

Distributed in the UK, Europe, South Africa and Asia
by TBS Ltd, TBS Distribution Centre, Colchester Road
Frating Green, Colchester CO7 7DW

This edition published in Australia in 2006
by Allen & Unwin Pty Ltd,
PO Box 8500, 83 Alexander Street,
Crows Nest, NSW 2065

Distributed in Canada by
Penguin Books Canada,
90 Eglinton Avenue East,
Suite 700, Toronto,
Ontario M4P 2YE

ISBN 10: 1-84046-754-1
ISBN 13: 978-1840467-54-3

Text copyright © 2005 Dixe Wills

The author has asserted his moral rights.

Maps reproduced by permission of the Ordnance Survey on behalf of the
Controller of HM Stationery Office, Crown copyright © 100044040

No part of this book may be reproduced in any form, or by any
means, without prior permission in writing from the publisher.

Design by Phillip Appleton
Crests designed by Oliver Pugh

Printed and bound in the UK by Creative Print and Design Group

'Zeal Farm is immediately to your left,
a blank canvas for your brilliant mind.'

CONTENTS

CONTENTS

USUAL CAVEAT

All the particulars in this guide are unerringly factual and, at time of going to press, are as much like facts as can be had, the only exception to this rule being the claim that during the winter months Zeal Farm (Somerset) is twice the size of Wales. Change is, of course, the stuff of life, and the author takes no responsibility for the consequent down-scaling of any facts herein to the status of retro-facts, fiction or out-and-out falsehoods. Furthermore, any injuries incurred by you while using this guide are clearly your fault, as are any inaccuracies, misprints, errors, omissions or typographical blunders. The author has half a mind to sue.

FOREWORD

'Show me the least considered corner of a man's soul and I will show you the man.' Noé Xiste (1695-1735)

Admittedly your life *is* horrible. The sheer awfulness of your existence is something far beyond the scope of human imagining. I'm sorry about it, of course, but there's very little I can do. Close your eyes though, if you can, to the relentless tragedy that pervades your every waking moment and imagine for a second what life is like for the letter *z*.

Not for it the lisping sibilant exuberance of the *f* or the seemingly perpetual popularity of the garrulous *e*. No one will ever say of it '… and last but not least …'. For not only is *z* the final letter of all, it's also the most seldom called upon by the English tongue, less frequented even than exotics like *q* and *x*. It skulks at the tail of the alphabet and buzzes fitfully like a fridge of its own making.

Regrettably, the same fate is inevitably shared by those places in Britain which, for better or worse, have pluckily elected to invert the established order of things by declaring that the last shall be first. Zabulon, Zeals, Zouch – all have swum against the tide of linguistic convention. Dorset's

Zig Zag Hill, indeed, flaunts two of the little chaps with a recklessness that borders on abandon. Is it just coincidence that such a place is left an uninhabited desert, shunned by the neighbouring populace of smug zedless Shaftesbury?

This guide, then, is an attempt to bat on the side of the underdog, a beast whose middle-order frailties are only too well documented. The traveller who takes the trouble to follow its lead through the pavilion of ignominious defeat and off the beaten track will be rewarded by encounters with places for the most part unsullied by the depredations of modern life and wholly undisturbed by any pretensions to greatness. Just like the French Revolution: to be alive there is very heaven.

In order to extract every last tuft of wool from the z goat, there can be found in these pages a handy rating system, specially designed crests, and the full story of the pivotal role played in the English Civil War by each of the 41 locales. All the remaining information has been plucked from choice trees of knowledge for the sole purpose of enhancing the enjoyment of your visit to a pitch which, given good weather conditions, should oscillate between delight and mild hysteria.

The one true adventure may well be the journey into self, but it is well known that it's a hazardous thing to send a postcard from the core of your very being. A visit to the site of a z, on the other hand, is not only a celebration of the great unsung, but the beginning of a journey that has no end. Probably.

—⟨◇⟩—

INTRODUCTION

Earl of Kent (in a bit of a bate) to Oswald: 'Thou whorson zed! thou unnecessary letter!' William Shakespeare, *King Lear*

Glass for tin

The first zed ever uttered on British soil probably came out of the mouth of a man who had sailed all the way from what we now call Syria. Over 3,000 years ago, before London was even thought of, Phoenician traders were gallantly sailing all the way to western Britain to swap avant-garde glass products for chunks of tin. There's not a great deal of common ground between Phoenician (a Semitic language) and Cornish (a Celtic one), so one can only imagine that there was a lot of pointing and hand signals going on. Back then, the Cornish had no zed at all, so exposure to the *zayin* must have caused a bit of a rumpus, especially when they discovered what a prominent place it held in the Phoenician alphabet.

Meanwhile, down in Greece, the locals had borrowed this same alphabet, presumably promising to return it in a few weeks, and set about adapting it to their own needs. As a consequence they soon developed a fondness for what they called *zeta*, which they pronounced *dz*. There followed an extraordinary bout of cheating, with the Etruscans copying the alphabet off the Greeks and the Romans copying off the Etruscans until eventually everyone's homework looked exactly the same. Unfortunately, the Romans didn't really know what to do with the *zeta* since no one in Rome ever felt the need to say *dz*, at least not outside the vomitorium. Therefore, although the letter came in at no. 7 in the Roman alphabet, after a while they decided they couldn't really be doing with it and it began to trail in 23rd and last.

Region

Worse was to come. In 312 BC the official censor, Appius Claudius Caecus, abolished the zed altogether and replaced it with a *g* — a decision not quite as biggare as it may at first appear if you consider words like 'beige' and 'rouge' — and it certainly didn't prevent the Romans from becoming top dog in the region and plundering flash words for abstract concepts from the cultured Athenians. Nevertheless, it took until the 1st century AD before they grudgingly reintroduced the zed, and even then it was mainly to stop the Greeks from laughing at them for mis-spelling their words. Just to make sure the returnee knew its place, though, it was tacked on to the end of the alphabet after johnny-come-lately *y*, and the Roman scholar Martius dismissed it as a 'double hissing sound'.

It was around this time that the Romans first became acquainted with the singularities of the British climate and thoughtfully brought their alphabet along with them to amuse themselves during the eleven months a year when it rained. This was the island's first prolonged exposure to the letter zed but it never really took off and the arrival of Saxon guests on British soil with their almost completely zedless language hardly furthered the cause. The Vikings had a rune that was roughly equivalent to a zed but no one much took to runes either. It seems that in that awkward spell when the years ran to only three digits, the preference of ordinary people was to deal with any sound that approximated a zed by taking it round the back of a dark bailey and garrotting it, the weapon of choice being the flexible and accommodating *s*.

Fangled

It was not until the arrival of William the Conqueror in 1066 that the zed began to be used in Britain with any frequency and even then it hardly received a rapturous reception. The Normans, however, enjoyed a good zed and so one can only imagine their chagrin when the locals preferred to repeat history and render the new-fangled sound as a *g*, or even an *i*, the capital of which does at least resemble a *ʒ*

Ha' done

Five centuries later and the zed still held such a lowly position in the English language that Shakespeare's only use for it was as an insult. It was not even guaranteed an inclusion in dictionaries of the time and was often replaced by *ss*. This hand-to-mouth existence is illustrated by the fact that no one could quite remember its name. It was variously known as zad, zard, ezod, uzzard, izzard and izard — the lengthier versions probably stemming from the French practice of saying 'et zède' at the end of a recital of the alphabet. (There was nothing the 17th-century Frenchman enjoyed more of an evening than a good get-together around the fire for some rousing alphabet recitals. Some of the professional *alphabéteurs* were even able to commit the entire thing to memory.)

Since then, the zed has hung on grimly to the coat-tails of the English alphabet, often joined by non-letters such as & and bits of stray punctuation. Indeed, there have been times when the general feeling has been that zed had even less right to be there than such scratches and splodges. In George Eliot's novel *Adam Bede*, Jacob Storey comments: 'He thought it [z] had only been put to finish off th' alphabet like; though *ampusand* would ha' done as well, for what he could see.'

Even in today's free-wheeling Rabelaisian Britain, zed is

still the least used letter in everyday English. It only ever drags itself out of last place of any league table you care to throw at it if you take the trouble to count the letters occurring in every single entry in the dictionary, in which case it just manages to haul itself fractionally above q and j.

Any

However, it should be remembered that English is not the only language spoken in Britain. Unfortunately, none of the Celtic languages that adorn the isle — Welsh, Scots Gaelic and Cornish — has ever felt much need to bother with a zed except *in extremis*. It may seem perplexing therefore that no fewer than thirteen of the entries in this guide are found in Cornwall.[1] This is explained by a deeply pleasing glitch in the geo-linguistic continuum. Celtic languages are subject to something called mutation. In a nutshell, this means that certain letters of words change according to the position of the word in the sentence. By a curious idiosyncrasy whose origins are, at best, hazy, in Cornish an s will sometimes mutate to a z. Quirkier still, this happens only with place names. As a result, the Cornish — who, as we have seen, were the very first on the island to encounter the zed in any form — have rather fittingly ended up with the most significant concentration of place names that begin with the letter.

Thin

As for the remainder, they have come down to us by a variety of ways. Some have appropriated their names from people; others have thumbed the silky pages of the Bible for inspiration; some have corrupted Old English or Latin words; one derives its name from a man-made feature; some commemorate historical events; while the genesis of a few has been so dissolved by the acid rains of time that we can only peer at them through painfully squinting eyes and speculate while our companions, their patience already worn perilously thin, yawn noisily and look at their watches. Perhaps, in the end, it *is* time to go after all.

---

[1] The western-centric distribution of zeds has, of course, produced its share of hoax theories such as the now notorious Selbst Vacuum Theory (SVT). This hypothesis, which it should be pointed out has never existed in any form, posits the supposition that zeds were susceptible to a vacuum created by the movement of the seas over Zantman's Rock and have thus been dragged south-westwards towards it. With no other theories, extant or imaginary, to challenge this proposition, Selbst became the accepted truth, albeit one that could not itself exist in a vacuum. Inevitably, it didn't take long before a rift emerged among the followers of Selbst between the *Stasisists* – who believed that the zeds, having been sucked down, became stable – and the *Continuumists* – who asserted that the vacuum was still drawing the zeds towards it and that in several thousand years' time all the zeds would have joined together just west of the Scilly Isles to form an enormous super-zed that would explode, causing tiny zed droplets to form thousands of new islets in the Atlantic. Thankfully, none of this really matters much, though the rift has regrettably been the cause of several outbreaks of fisticuffs between the opposing parties and led to the so-called Vacuum Riots in Surrey in the 1920s.

GUIDE TO THE GUIDE

Getting maximum mileage from this book – using it, abusing it, swallowing a page a day as a protest against some as yet undefined injustice.

Here's what you can expect to encounter:

42
Zulforth Plethora

Number and name of Z. Numbers in numerical order, names in alphabetical order

– just like the universe as described by Kant.

A handy crest designed especially to commemorate all the elements that make the locale unique and special, even in the event of it being incalculably tedious or as dreary as a day spent in someone else's custard.

An at-a-glance guide to each location's picturesqueness,

Picturesqueness	3/6
Acuity	2/6
Slant	1/6

acuity and slant. Knowledge is power. Subjective opinion is the new Knowledge.

Proof positive from our friends at the Ordnance Survey that the Z in question really exists. Also places the Z in the context of surrounding features such as space, ground, and bits of land where nothing much happens.

Why's it called that?: Yes, why? Good question.

Where is it?: Useful, though still rather hazy notions concerning a Z's location.

Where exactly?: Less vague, more utilitarian information on geographical positioning.

No, where *exactly*?: Guidance to placate even the most exacting pedant.

Population: Mock if you like, but if you live to 50, one in four of these people will be related to you at some point in your life.

Getting there: Simply jump on a train with your tricycle and follow these ambiguous, obtuse, and often deliberately unintelligible instructions. Discover the exact depth of your resolve (fathoms to metres conversion chart included).

What's there?: What to expect.

Things to do: What is expected of you in return.

Things to look out for: What offers more satisfaction in life than the garnering of points? Each of the 41 Zs offers three chances to scoop them up — that's 123 opportunities to prove yourself the greatest human being in all of creation.

Nearest pub: A chance to relax in good company and fine surroundings. If there is no such chance you can always hazard a visit to the nearest pub.

Nearest public phone box: Even though we may not even admit it to ourselves, mobile phones are clearly a fad. Which of us in five years' time will be seen dead with one of these miniature bleating boxes of control freakery? Certainly not you. Get to know a phone box and it will repay you into all eternity.

Nearest body of water: An autumn of ever warming global relations almost inevitably leads to a nuclear winter. When the bomb drops, a man's best friend is water. A woman's best friend is also water. A child's best friend is Mikey the Monkey. This is why no children will survive a nuclear holocaust.

What's furry?: What lives there? What comes and goes? Does it mistakenly say 'regular' when it means 'frequent'?

What lives in the green bins?: Glass, paper, tin or kedgeree?

Role in Civil War: Life is a civil war. Learn from the mistakes of the past.

Claim to fame: Celebrity is dead. Hurrah.

Killer fact: Memorise it. Bring it out in the evenings. Silence your friends.

WARNING

In a hundred years' time, Britain will be a proletarian utopia in which not only the tools of production but also the entire land mass of the nation will be in the control of the workers. Until then, please do respect the property and land belonging to those who live in the places described in this guide and keep in mind that they probably wish to meet you much less than you wish to meet them.

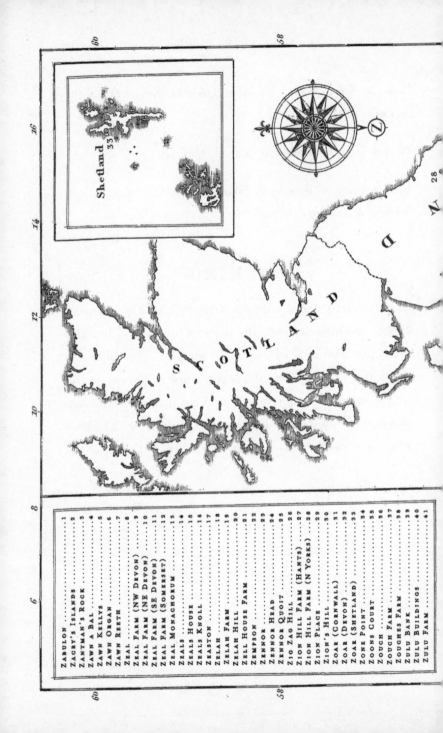

Shetland

SCOTLAND

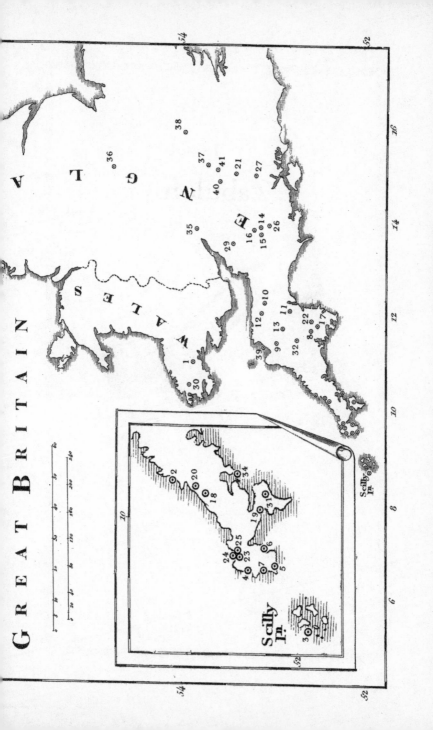

1

Zabulon

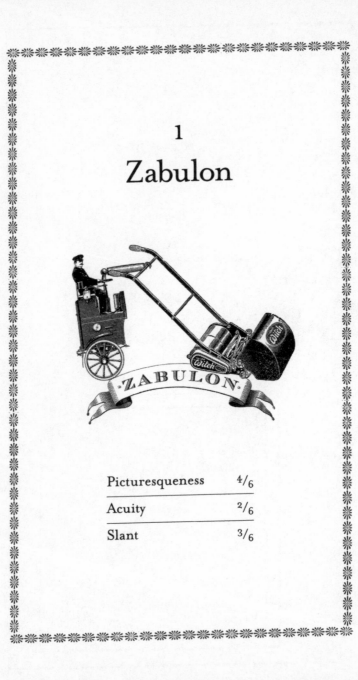

Picturesqueness	$^4/_6$
Acuity	$^2/_6$
Slant	$^3/_6$

Why's it called that?: Derived from the Hebrew name for one of the sons of Jacob and hence one of the tribes of Israel. Also gets a mention in Matthew 4:13: 'And leaving Nazareth, he came and dwelt in Capernaum, which is upon the sea coast, in the borders of Zabulon and Nephthalim'; and Revelation 7:8: 'Of the tribe of Zabulon were sealed twelve thousand.' The farm, population somewhat less than twelve thousand, was originally spelt Sabulon but got changed to Zabulon (fig. 2), presumably in a doomed bid to appear windswept and exotic.

Fig. 1.

Where is it?: Not so far from St Clears (Sanclêr, Welshily), Carmarthenshire (Sir Gaerfyrddin), Wales (Cymru), oh yes it is (o do dydy).

Where exactly?: OS Landranger Map 158: SN2416 (fig. 1).

No, where *exactly*?: The Ordnance Survey *Gazetteer of Great Britain* locates the hamlet at Latitude 51°49.1'N Longitude 4°32.8'W, whereas the merest flick of an eye at a map is enough to know it's evidently much more like 51°49.15'N 4°33.12'W, a good three-quarters of a mile away. Who is there left to trust?

Population: 2 + sundry animals including two dogs, one called Tim, the other one not.

Getting there: Take the train to Whitland (on Sundays you may have to bring your own) then strike east along the B4328. Slink onto a little yellow road for a bit, before joining the capacious but surly A40 for a few hundred yards. Turn first right onto a comforting little

Fig. 2.

yellow road again, nip under the railway bridge and it's second on your right.

What's there?: A cattle farm (some sheep, some cats) comprising 193 acres of land; a big farmhouse (fig. 3); a kitchen garden; a sit-on lawnmower; a pond; and some sheds, barns and certain other farm buildings in which eclectic farm-like things go on, the mysteries of which are not to be pondered on by the city-dweller.

Fig. 3.

Things to do: Look at cattle. Look at sheep. Look at duckweed in the pond. Plunge into pond riding sit-on lawnmower. Weep.

THINGS TO LOOK OUT FOR

Fig. 4.

Fig. 5.

☞ *Sheep, attentive* (fig. 4) — 1 POINT.

Sheep, cavalier (fig. 5) — 2 POINTS.

Daffodils, blasé yet reassuringly demotic (fig. 6) — 3 POINTS. ☜

Nearest pub: The White Lion in Pwll-trap (1¾ miles as the lawnmower trundles) is the nearest watering hole since the hamlet's own Cefyl du (The Black Horse) was tragically closed down in the 1800s.

Nearest public phone box: In the shadow of The White Lion in Pwll-trap, position of the sun permitting (1¾ miles east — The White Lion, that is, not the sun, which is considerably further away, even on days when it's really hot).

Fig. 6.

Nearest body of water: Some say the Afon Taf while others claim its tributary the Afon Fenni is closer. You decide who's telling the truth and who is pitifully misguided or, quite possibly, just wilfully dishonest.

What's furry?: Cats, sheep, daffodils, though the food chain is not necessarily in that order.

What lives in the green bins?: The *Western Telegraph*: 'The newspaper that fights for Pembrokeshire' (may contain blood stains).

Role in Civil War: One-time Parliamentarian Rowland Laugharne — whose surname is celebrated by a village five miles south-east of Zabulon — joined a revolt against his paymasters in 1648. The colonel marched several thousand Pembrokeshire men eastwards, probably passing very close to the farm. A week or so later he was back, this time fleeing westwards after being trounced by Cromwell just outside Cardiff. Eventually captured and condemned to death along with two fellow turncoats, Laugharne was spared the firing squad by an unorthodox attempt at a divine lottery in which a blind child drew papers out of a hat to determine their fate. The one drawn for Laugharne read 'Life given by God', and accordingly he was sent into exile. Some years later he returned to become an MP. This goes to show that there are some fates worse than death.

Claim to fame: Thomas Lewis, acclaimed missionary to The Congo, chose to preach his first ever sermon in the kitchen of the farmhouse at Zabulon. Doubtless someone took him aside later and told him all about churches and pulpits.

Killer fact: A large 'panther-like' animal has been spotted by primary school staff in a field near Whitland, a whisker or two from Zabulon, and is apparently still at large. Panthers are leopards, as any primary school teacher will tell you, and black panthers are merely leopards with melanism, though what we now know as cheetahs were once called leopards, which people used to think were a cross between a lion and a panther. Tsh. Panthers are not half as speedy as cheetahs but they are famously strong, enabling them to lift carcasses weighing over ten stone and plop them onto branches of trees twenty feet above the ground. If you do not wish your lifeless body to be lofted into a tree in Zabulon, you might want to consider putting on very heavy clothes before setting out.

1st July

Weather: Hail, some fatal

2

Zacry's Islands

Picturesqueness	$5/6$
Acuity	$5/6$
Slant	$6/6$

Why's it called that?: For a place whose name is mired in the quaggy fens of unrecorded history, Zacry's Islands has managed to pick up a healthy array of variants, including Zachry's, Zachory's and Zichory. More upsettingly, there's a certain uncertainty as to whether Zacry put his name to just the one island or to both the lumps of rock at the southern end of Tregurrian Beach. The weight of historical evidence comes down on the side of the plural form of the name, despite the modern predilection for the singular. Who Zacry was, and what his relationship with the islands might have been, are questions best left for those whose own questions have been taken from them.

Where is it?: On the southern end of Tregurrian Beach. Unhappily, the upset and uncertainty continue with the naming of the beach. Some favour Tregurrian, others Watergate. The world is full of care and trouble.

Where exactly?: OS Landranger Map 200: SW8363 (fig. 1).

No, where *exactly*?: The Cornish coast.

Population: 0.

Fig. 1.

Getting there: Bounce gaily out of Newquay station as if deaf to the crumps, clatters and clangs of the unseemly appellatory scuffling further along the coast. For you, hullabaloo is just a word to rhyme with gnu. Cyclists will need to take roads from here, but walkers have the delight of following the coastal path the whole 1½ miles to the islands. Waving the lucky walkers good morrow, as if you

Fig. 2.

bore them no ill will at all, turn right out of the station, press eastwards along the A3058, strike left down the B3276, pass Porth Beach, up the hill and, leaving the road behind, take the steps down to Whipsiderry Beach (fig. 6). Head north, having first checked the times of the tide carefully so as not to hasten unduly your passing to fresh pastures, pleasant though they say death by drowning can be. Zacry's are the two big islands on the beach (fig. 2) that are probably at least a bit in the sea, if not entirely in it. If they are entirely in it, you didn't read the tide timetable correctly. Retreat is preferable to regret.

What's there?: Two rocks. Some sea. Some beach. Less is more.

Things to do: Clamber. Scramble. Topple. Lie on your back, feel the sun on your face, hear the wind whipping the grass, and wonder why you so rarely ever do this.

THINGS TO LOOK OUT FOR

☞ *Mussels on a rock (serving suggestion only)* (fig. 4) – 3 POINTS.

Basking cliff (fig. 3) – 1 POINT.

The question at the centre of the universe (fig. 5) – 2 POINTS (Warning: Those who decide to wander barefoot through the sandy shallows to the other end should be wary of loose interrogatives.) ✍

Fig. 3.

Nearest pub: The Mermaid Inn, Porth Beach. The Gull Rock Hotel claims to be a pub and is even closer than the Mermaid but is, on inspection, a hotel bar. The difference is subtle but immense.

Nearest public phone box: At the entrance to the Porth Beach Tourist Park, which sounds worse than it is.

Nearest body of water: Watergate Bay. As far as can be ascertained, this is its only name.

Fig. 4.

What's furry?: Grass, gulls, oystercatchers, oysters (presumably), limpets, mussels, indeterminate sea-snaily things whose names are known only to the children in Enid Blyton books.

What lives in the green bins?: Ozone, salt.

Role in Civil War: The islands' steepness does not make them conducive to mass cavalry charges which is probably why they survived the war more or less unscathed. In fact, this whole corner of Cornwall got off pretty lightly, assuming of course that you don't count the thousands of men who went off to fight on behalf of the King and then failed to make it home again.

Fig. 5.

Claim to fame: Iron Age man — so called because his shirts were always really smooth — was forever trampling around these parts and even took the trouble of building a fort at the other end of Whipsiderry Beach and experimenting with the smelting of iron.

Killer fact: Bronze Age man — so called because he was rarely seen without an exceptional tan — was forever dying in these parts, mainly from iron-smelting accidents, and

Fig. 6.

even took the trouble of burying himself in two barrows still clearly visible on the cliff-tops directly above Zacry's right island.

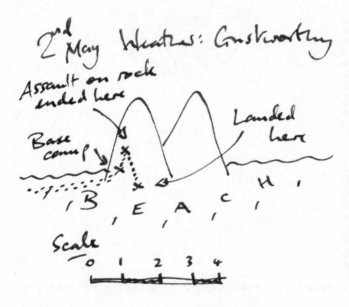

3
Zantman's Rock

Picturesqueness	6/6
Acuity	6/6
Slant	4/6

Why's it called that?: Ask ten passing cormorants and you'll get ten different answers. Of course, your chances of interpreting any of them accurately are on the scrawny side of slim, much like the evidence for the Dutchman who lent his name to the rock after, possibly, being shipwrecked and finding himself in the unenviable position of clinging on to it. Doubly unenviable, in fact, because twice a day the rock is completely submerged. However, since we know this hypothetical sailor's name, the chances are that he lived to tell his hypothetical rescuers what it was, unless of course they just found it written inside his hypothetical breeches when he was washed up on the shore the following day. Anyway, the name Zantman's Rock is recorded on an Admiralty chart of 1860. Before then, it appears not to have been distinguished from the Crim Rocks which lurk just to

the south, so any clinging that took place probably did so in the 19th century, though not, obviously, for much of it.

Where is it?: Off the Scilly Isles, a bit to the north of the Bishop Rock lighthouse.

Where exactly?: OS Landranger Map 203: SV8009 (fig. 1).

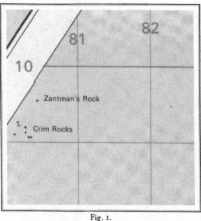

Fig. 1.

No, where *exactly*?: At low tide, as far to the south-west of Britain as you can possibly be without being in the sea.

Population: 0 (may have been inhabited, briefly, once).

Getting there: From Penzance station, stroll southwards to Lighthouse Pier. Board the *Scillonian III* (one a day, more or less, except in the low season, and rarely on Sundays), chug for 2½ hours. Disembark at Hugh Town, the immense sprawling capital of St Mary's isle. Depending on your proficiency with a cutlass, either commandeer or charter a boat to take you the five nautical miles west-south-west to Zantman's Rock. (Please note, however, that piracy is still illegal in fuddy-duddy Britain, even for the purposes of research.)

Fig. 2.

What's there?: A huge lump of granite. Unfortunately not quite so huge as to form anything useful like an island or even a decent-sized ledge on which things that get used only occasionally but which still need to be more or less to hand could be put, but still huge enough to be a nuisance to shipping.

Things to do: Cling.

THINGS TO LOOK OUT FOR

☞ *The rock, close up, as Zantman himself may have seen it* (fig. 3) – 1 POINT.

The same rock, a bit later, not quite so inviting (fig. 4) – 1 POINT.

The Bishop Rock Lighthouse – a longer swim than it looks (fig. 2) – 1 POINT. ✍

Nearest pub: The Turk's Head, St Agnes' isle. Britain's most south-westerly Customs

Fig. 3.

Fig. 4.

House is now its most south-westerly pub.

Nearest public phone box: On St Agnes, just along from the post office. Agnes was about twelve or thirteen when she was executed by the Romans by being stabbed in the throat. Try not to think about this too much when making calls.

Nearest body of water: The Atlantic. Too darn near at times.

>•<

What's furry?: Cormorants, black redstarts, storm petrels, Manx shearwaters and the occasional dazed upland (Bartram's) sandpiper.

What lives in the green bins?: Breeches, cutlasses, guano.

Role in Civil War: The Cavaliers surrendered the Scilly Isles, Zantman's Rock and all, in 1646 but rebelled two years later to find themselves in the unenviable position (see hypothetical Dutch sailor, above) of being the very last Royalist stronghold in Britain. Before this, Prince Charles had the good sense to hole up on the isles when all was lost in England. Had he known that a few short years later the isle of Tresco would have a castle named after his arch-nemesis Cromwell, he might well have thrown in the kerchief and gone to live with the Pope or something instead of mooching around Europe whining endlessly and combing his hair while waiting for the Republic to fail.

Claim to fame: The wreck of the *Thornliebank* lies just off the rock. The full-rigged sailing ship made an unscheduled visit in dense fog at 5 a.m. on 28 November 1913 on its way from Pisagua to Falmouth. Happily, the crew managed to get themselves to safety in a lifeboat but the ship and cargo – nitrate of soda – went to the bottom. The ship's bell has been recovered but the Atlantic has, by all reports, made something of a mess of everything else.

>•<

Killer fact: Travelling west from the rock, the first land you come across is the United States of America, a country that used to be owned by Britain but which fell into disuse.

13th April   Weather: Scorchful

Thomliebank

Nitrate of soda

Scale (fathoms)

Fathomable   0   Unfathomable

The endless sea of regret is best travelled in a catamaran -
Tacitus

4

Zawn a Bal

Picturesqueness	4/6
Acuity	3/6
Slant	6/6

Why's it called that?: Derived from the Cornish 'Saven-an-bal', in which 'saven' means 'cleft', 'a' can be handily fudged as 'of the', and 'bal' is 'mine'. Thus 'Cleft of the Mine', which sounds like it should be a folk song. This turns out to be somewhat apt, given Zawn a Bal's close relationship with the big-jumpered acoustic art. The cleft in question is one in the cliffs; the mine the one underneath.

Where is it?: In Cornwall. Almost off Cornwall, in fact.

Where exactly?: OS Landranger Map 203: SW3633 (fig. 1).

No, where _exactly_?: So tantalisingly close to being owned by the National Trust that it practically has its own tea-towel.

Population: 0.

Getting there: From Penzance station, fashion a left along the A30, head through town

Fig. 1.

and scurry right onto the A3071. This takes you all the way to St Just who, in a perfect world, would be the Patron Saint of Having About Enough But No More. Carry on along the B3306 to Botallack. In the village, take a left past the Queen's Arms and, where the road suddenly

Fig. 2.

resembles a blackbird's tail at rest, carry straight on and head for the chimney (fig. 2).

What's there?: A zawn, a bal. In a perfect world – one in which the benign theocracy of St Just gave to each purpose and to all a sense of belonging – that would be everything. However, a tin mine is seldom just a tin mine, especially when its ore contains a lot of arsenic. Hence the existence of the arsenic chimney, arsenic calciner and arsenic labyrinth where worked the women and children. They didn't do it for long, mind, preferring to die painfully instead.

Things to do: Breathe in. Breathe out. Expire.

Fig. 3.

◆

THINGS TO LOOK OUT FOR

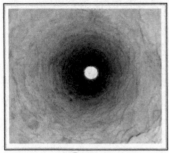

Fig. 2a.   Fig. 4.

☞ *Arsenic labyrinth* (fig. 3) — 2 POINTS.

Arsenic chimney (figs 2 & 2a) — 2 POINTS.

The Crowns engine houses — they're famous apparently, like so much else (fig. 4) — 2 POINTS. ☜

Nearest pub: The Queen's Arms, Botallack, a village of some considerable ugliness — as if a great jumble of houses had been tossed to earth and all the nice ones had fallen into the sea.

Nearest public phone box: In Carnyorth, opposite the Outdoor Education Centre (which, perversely, appears to be indoors).

Nearest body of water: Some zawns have streams running down them. Not this one. However, in common with most coastal features, the sea is seldom far away (fig. 5).

What's furry?: Chiffchaffs, guillemots, lungs.

◆

Fig. 5.

What lives in the green bins?: A sadness normally only associated with Belgians.

Role in Civil War: Tin was absurdly important in the war because you could make so many things out of it, like tins. It was also an excellent material if you were partial to a bit of rust. Cornwall took the Royalist side throughout the conflict, which explains why the Roundheads were so envious of the Cavaliers' conspicuous display of rust whenever the two met to do battle.

Claim to fame: The zawn boasts competing claims exactly a century apart. In 1865 the Prince and Princess of Wales dropped by on a visit to what was once Cornwall's richest tin mine. No doubt inspired by this, the mine's resident folk group released an album in 1965 that included a lament for the passing of corporal punishment and/or sugar and/or insubstantial furniture, 'There Ain't No More Cane'.

Killer fact: Since the mine's seams went far out under the sea, it was apparently not uncommon for terrified miners to retreat at full pelt with the waves crashing a few feet above their heads.

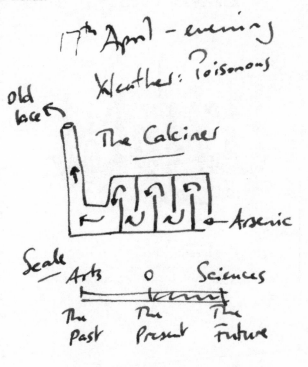

5
Zawn Kellys

Picturesqueness	$6/6$
Acuity	$3/6$
Slant	$5/6$

Why's it called that?: Zawn, as usual, comes from the Cornish word 'saven' meaning a cleft, while Kellys is a short step from 'kelli', a grove. Sadly, although there's still quite clearly a cleft here, the grove is long gone, much like the word itself.

Where is it?: At the end of England. That's if you think of Cornwall as England, of course. Most Cornish people don't. They have their own flag and everything. It's like the Cross of St George except that the white is black and the red is white. It's piratical and mysterious and the height of separatist chic.

Where exactly?: OS Landranger Map 203: SW3522 (fig. 1).

No, where *exactly*?: Where the unstoppable waters of the Atlantic meet the immovable granite of Cornwall. Just like a bad soap powder commercial, really, except that the granite doesn't emerge a white that's whiter and fresher than ever before.

Population: 0.

Getting there: Follow the directions to Zawn Reeth as far as Bosistow. The track gives up just short of Zawn Kellys so you'll have to make your way south along a footpath from

Fig. 1.

there. A more enriching
experience can be had if,
rather than turning off to
Bosistow, you carry straight
on to Porthgwarra. After the
last house, bear right
towards what the Ordnance

Fig. 2.

Survey insists is a Mountain Rescue Post despite the fact
that the nearest mountain is over 150 miles away in South
Wales. Chuckle to yourself as you wave to the men in the
Coastal Watch Station while feigning an injury caused by a
loose crampon. From here, take the path north-west
through a gap in an ancient wall and onwards until a rock
on the forecliffs lines up with a cave on the far side of
Pendower Coves (fig. 3). At this point, turn sharply towards
the sea and in no time you'll be at the head of the zawn.

Fig. 3.

Fig. 4.

What's there?: A cliff, a cleft, a dribble of water, the sigh of an evanescent grove, a shadow.

Things to do: Decide to descend the zawn to the sea, which looks so nice today. Get halfway down to the bit where it unexpectedly gets very steep. Decide that the sea is, after all, looking a bit choppy.

THINGS TO LOOK OUT FOR

☞ *A daymark — it tells seafarers where they are during the day. At night, it allows seafarers to plough cheerfully into the cliffs* (**fig. 2**) — 2 POINTS.

Longship's Lighthouse — it tells seafarers where they are at night. By day, it allows

Fig. 5.

seafarers to plough cheerfully onto the rocks (**fig. 5**) — 2 POINTS.

Zawn Kellys — ploughing actively encouraged, day or night. No coaches (**figs 4 & 4a**) — 1 POINT. ✒

Fig. 4a.

Nearest pub: Sennen's The First and Last, which, as the name suggests, is the first and last pub in Sennen.

Nearest public phone box: In Porthgwarra — especially useful if you hazard upon any mountains that need rescuing.

Nearest body of water: A brook topples headlong down the zawn as if gravity were the only truth.

What's furry?: The three-cornered leek, the wild carrot, the sea carrot, the tormentil.

What lives in the green bins?: Bark. Danger. Separatism.

Role in Civil War: Just what use a zawn is in times of war is debatable. Certainly, neither side managed to come up with any means of using this one to their advantage. In retrospect, perhaps that's a good thing.

Claim to fame: This particular cleft in the cliffs felt the thud and yaw of many an ancient Briton, as evidenced by the fort that tops Carn Lês Boel at the other end of Pendower Coves. It's tempting to think that the fort served as a predecessor to the Minack, an amphitheatre carved out of the cliffs just round the coast. Unfortunately, it's also ludicrous and typical of the way modern observers romanticise the past in order to make it less frightening.

Killer fact: Not all the zawns that exist make it into the Ordnance Survey's *Gazetteer*. Those with more time than they know what to do with, or no friends, or both, might scour the Cornish coast for Zawn Vinoc, Zawn Buzz and Gen, Zawn South, Zawn Varrap, Zawn Susan, Zawn Gamper, Zawn Trevilley, Zawn Wells, Zawn Duel and Zawn Quoits. Those with friends might want to take a friend along.

17th April – afternoon
Weather: Unseemly
List of Things
Sugar
Flour
Blackcurrant jam
The sound of my own name
echoing into eternity
Cornflour
Plums

6

Zawn Organ

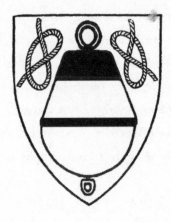

Picturesqueness	5/6
Acuity	3/6
Slant	5/6

Why's it called that?: The zawn bit, as is the case with the other zawns, is the Cornish for 'cleft'. The organ bit is more problematic since on close inspection it becomes quite clear that there is no organ here, nor ever was probably. There is, however, a good deal of organic material and it would be satisfying to think that this, or the notable lack of pesticides used in the area, was responsible for the name. Sadly, as with a good deal that might prove satisfying in life, this is unlikely.

Where is it?: To the south of Penzance.

Where exactly?: OS Land-ranger Map 203: SW4624 (fig. 1).

No, where *exactly*?: In a cliff, beneath some nature.

Population: 0.

Fig. 1.

Getting there: From Penzance station, hug the coastal road south, gulping in views of St Michael's Mount. The road passes through Newlyn before arriving at Mousehole (pron. 'm-owzul'), though devotees of top beat combo The Beatles may wish to take the inland road through Paul (pron. 'rin-go') instead. Where the road leading south out of Mousehole turns sharply right (just over the giant 'mouse hole' in the cliffs below which lends its name to the village; it's really quite impressive seen from the sea — one fully expects a giant mouse to emerge from it and cause havoc by descending on the village and scaring all its elephants), turn left onto the coastal path. Wander along here for a bit, passing an old look-out post, crossing a stream and entering the Kemyel Crease nature reserve. Just after leaving the reserve at the southern end there is a deeply dangerous informal path

Fig. 2.

plunging down to the sea. Do not plunge down into the sea yourself unless you too are a path. In fact, it would be inadvisable to do anything but stare at this path in disbelief. Should you find yourself somehow at the bottom of it, get up and double back over the rocks towards an inlet. There is a hole at the foot of the cliff. Voilà! Zawn Organ.

What's there?: An inlet, a hole, some cliff, the Buoy of Significance.

Things to do: Look at the hole. Chances are there will be some water running out of it. Water is always fun. Interact with the Buoy of Significance. It is pink with a tuft of blue rope like two braids of hair dyed with woad. It symbolises the feminisation of Ancient British culture under Boadicea. Ancient Britons are always fun.

THINGS TO LOOK OUT FOR

☞ *The inlet* (fig. 2) – 1 POINT.

The Buoy of Significance (fig. 3) – 2 POINTS.

The Buoy of Significance vaulting meaningfully in front of the zawn (fig. 4) – 5 POINTS. ✑

Fig. 3.

Fig. 4.

Nearest pub: It would be tempting to believe that Mousehole's The Ship Inn was Zawn Organ's nearest house of bevvery, but closer by some margin, to the dismay and anger of those who claim some authority in the matter, is the Lamorna Wink (fig. 5), tucked away in the close confines of the valley to which it owes its name.

Nearest public phone box: Authorities on the matter are apt to become further enraged when faced with incontrovertible proof that the nearest phone box is not the one across the road from The Ship Inn but rather the one next to Lamorna village hall. Furthermore, for a small fee, you can hire the hall — the perfect opportunity to exhibit

Fig. 5.

that peerless collection of eyebrows you've got stuffed in boxes in the spare room.

Nearest body of water: Not the sea, as might be supposed by the casual aqualogist, but the rivulet that flows down the zawn itself.

What's furry?: The roots of coniferous things.

What lives in the green bins?: Significance, meaning, purpose, worth.

Role in Civil War: One of the leaders of a Royalist uprising in May 1648 — during the so-called Second Civil War — was one William Keigwin of Mousehole. After a few days of some general plundering and looting in Penzance, the Sheriff turned up with 500 men and the fun was officially over. Keigwin might well have hidden in the zawn for a bit while things blew over.

Claim to fame: The land directly above Zawn Organ is not only a nature reserve but was also the scene of some audacious flower farming. In the early 20th century, terraced fields — known as quillels — were cut into the slope and bulbs planted to sprout in the morning sun.

Killer fact: During World War II, bulb production at Zawn Organ was switched to potatoes — a move many observers believe to have been the turning point in the conflict.

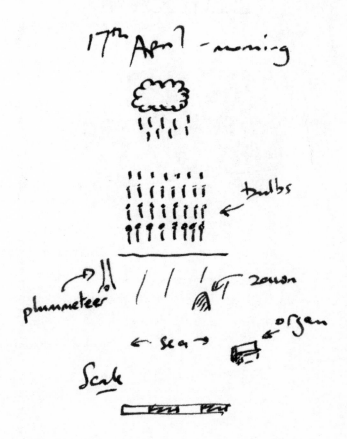

7
Zawn Reeth

Picturesqueness	$^6/_6$
Acuity	$^4/_6$
Slant	$^4/_6$

Why's it called that?: It's pretty flat as zawns go, but the Cornish word from which its name is derived still denotes 'a cleft', but more of this later. According to tradition, the latter word here is a corruption of 'rudh' and means 'red'. However, 'reeth' is more commonly a distortion of 'rydh' meaning 'free'. The cleft is certainly not all that red, even at sunset. On the other hand, you don't have to pay to see it, so tradition may not be the wise old owl we often take it for.

Where is it?: Nearer Land's End than you might care to hope or imagine.

Where exactly?: OS Landranger Map 203: SW3523 (fig. 1).

No, where _exactly_?: 874 miles from John O'Groats as the sponsor form crinkles.

Population: 0.

Getting there: Unfurl your-self at Penzance station and drift left onto the waiting A30. Hang a left at Catchall onto the B3283 and burrow through St Buryan, Treen —

Fig. 1.

a village accidentally named after the collective term for minor tableware carved from single pieces of wood — and finally Trethewey. Where the road kicks right at a crossroads of sorts, take a left and then first right through Lower Bosistow. Continue towards the sea, taking another right, and skipping left onto a path that falls below an impressively four-square sort of house. Where you encounter a little bridge, there also will be Zawn Reeth.

What's there?: A little bridge, a mysterious double wall, a flattish bit of stream and a dramatic cleft (fig. 2), but more of this later.

Fig. 2.

Things to do: Play a little bridge. Hypothesise wildly about the significance of the double wall. Become too too giddy with excitement. Start hyperventilating. Leave.

THINGS TO LOOK OUT FOR

☞ *Bridge (figures not supplied)* (fig. 3) — 1 POINT.

Double wall — a rare example of the short-lived craze for glass-free double-glazing (fig. 4) — 1 POINT.

Fig. 3.

Stream, not of conscious-ness but of water (fig. 5) — 1 POINT. ☜

Nearest pub: Shares Sennen's The First and Last with Zawn Kellys. Expect jostling.

Fig. 4.

Nearest public phone box: At Land's End. Not so much a telephone box as a telephone box experience.

Nearest body of water: The stream that passes through Zawn Reeth begins its brief life at two nearby springs. Imagine an 'OO' scale model of the Avon that someone has made vastly too small by accidentally putting a decimal point

Fig. 5.

in the wrong place. Each year, around the longest day, the decimal point reaches the mouth of the stream and dribbles into the sand. It's really quite moving.

What's furry?: Swallows – so many that if they inhabited the ground you'd walk to the sound of crunching swallow bones. As it is, there's a lot of manic swooping and plunging. One day they'll have someone's eye out and it will spoil it for everyone.

What lives in the green bins?: The desperation of non-fast cottons. An angling after something that was never intended.

Role in Civil War: Clefts were mightily under-used in the internecine struggle. The Roundheads preferred a good honest plain whereas the Cavaliers were always more partial to a knoll or a promontory. The only time sojourners at Zawn Reeth could feel involved was at the very end of the war when they could wave to various Royalist bigwigs, from Prince Charles down, as they passed in their ships bound for their last refuge, the Scilly Isles.

Claim to fame: Zawn Reeth marks the far eastern end of a little-known enigma. Tradition — which, as we have seen, is not always the nursemaid to Truth — dictates that there was once a rich and fertile land stretching all the way from Land's End to the Scilly Isles. It was peopled by the Silures — 'handsome maids and strong men' — and called Lyonesse. One hundred and forty villages stalked this land, each with its own church, set like gems around the exquisite city of Lions. In case this all seems a bit far-fetched and utopian, you should know that the *Chronicle of Florence of Worcester* gives the exact date — 11 November 1099 — that this land of milk and honey was undone by a freakishly high tide that caused the seas to o'errun it. Had the Domesday Book, compiled some thirteen years before this cataclysm, made any mention of the place at all, we'd doubtless all be listening out for the mournful tolling of the inundated church bells that can be heard on very calm days.

Killer fact: Draw a line in your mind's eye from the dramatic bit of the cleft to the feeble bit and it's not unreasonable to think that at one time the whole cleft was dramatic and that it's only because most of the outer rock has fallen away that the stream is left to flow tamely onto the beach.

17th April - mid-day   Weather: Calamitous

Scale   Here   There

8
Zeal

Picturesqueness	3/6
Acuity	5/6
Slant	2/6

Why's it called that?: Derived from its 12th-century name La Sele, 'sele' being the Old English for a sallow tree. However, some folk, for whom dull is evidently the new enchanting, sense that the name might come from a word meaning 'hall'.

Where is it?: Perched on the south-eastern corner of Dartmoor. There's nothing to the north or west but moor and attendant barrows, cairns, stone circles and other mysterious things best left alone.

Where exactly?: OS Landranger Map 202: SX6762 (fig. 1).

No, where *exactly*?: 50° 26.8'N 3° 52.0'W as the crow flies.

Population: About half a dozen, rising to a score or so if there are troubled Buddhists in town.

Getting there: Follow the instructions for Zempson (22), but at the final right-hand turn at the crossroads carry straight on through Har-bourneford. The roads from here on know not from logic, so take sandwiches and a trenching tool and be prepared to spend a good deal of the rest of your life aimlessly footling about until eventually

Fig. 1.

you forget why you came in the first place. It might be advisable at this point to give in, get married to a local person, settle down, have some children and await orders. In such circumstances, the following directions become a subject for mere intellectual stimulation which is distinctly preferable to having to rely on them for your survival. Take the second right, which comes ever so swiftly after the first right at a place where all the roads in history appear to

Fig. 2.

converge. After about a mile strike boldly left down a road that seems to be leading to where you've just come from. Carry straight on even though hacking a left would seem to feel more like

staying on the main road than staying on the main road actually feels. Do not be diverted by Overbrent, for this way only trouble lies. At the next junction you are faced with a choice disguised as a dilemma, for both ways are potentially correct. Flip a coin. Heads is left; tails is right; any other result should be ignored. Heads: cruise through Didworthy, at the T-junction forge a trail to your right, over Bala Brook, Zeal is your next stop. Tails: having taken a right, keep left at all costs unless you need a restorative ice cream at the little ice creamery on the right at Shipley Bridge.

Blunder through gates, cross cattle grids and, all things being well, Zeal will some day be yours.

What's there?: A sense of relief, mixed with a sense of achievement, mixed with a sense that you will never see home again. Also features a large cottage; a farm; and the Golden Buddha Centre, a retreat house for troubled Buddhists.

Things to do: Loaf about on Zeal Hill; do some farming; step into the river, while at the same time recognising that you cannot step into the same place twice.

THINGS TO LOOK OUT FOR

☞ *Golden Buddha Centre sign* (fig. 2) – 0 POINTS. Points are meaningless trivia. The only good is the extinction of self.

Zen arrangement of litter bins (fig. 3) – 1 POINT.

The steps of conundrum (fig. 4) – 1 POINT if you suspect they lead to nowhere; 5 POINTS if you come to the realisation that they lead to now here. ☜

Fig. 3.

Fig. 4.

Nearest pub: The Royal Oak (fig. 5), South Brent. If filled with day-trippers from Zempson, shuffle down the road to

Fig. 5.

The Packhorse to watch the lives of old men ebb away as they slouch in glum silence around the bar.

Nearest public phone box: Aish, just at the top of the hill, a vantage point from which you can see one county.

Nearest body of water: Bala Brook. Just to the south. If your coin landed on heads you will already have crossed it. If your coin landed on tails, you no longer know what water is.

What's furry?: Badgers, grass snakes, pipistrelles, and dormice (or 'brunch' as they're known to the other inhabitants).

What lives in the green bins?: The moment between was and is.

Role in Civil War: No soldier on either side who chanced upon Zeal was ever seen again. In this sense, the hamlet helped to curtail the war by reducing the number of men available to fight it.

Claim to fame: Little Zeal Cottage (fig. 6) was designed by a student of Lutyens and built in 1911 for George and Nora Townsend-Warner (the latter's ashes can still be found in the garden, though you probably wouldn't want to). Their daughter, Sylvia Townsend-Warner, was an author, poet and leading light in the Bloomsbury Set. She lived in the cottage with fellow wordflinger Valentine Ackland, and there wrote books on Tudor music and such treasured favourites as *Lolly Willowes*. This idyllic scene is only slightly tarnished by Sylvia's hatred for the cottage and her ceaseless complaints about having to live there.

Fig. 6.

Killer fact: Zeal's offspring include Zeal Hill, Zeal Plains, Zeal Pool, Zeal Gully, Zeal Burrows and that evergreen perennial Zeal Farm.

9

Zeal Farm (NW Devon)

Picturesqueness	$3/6$
Acuity	$2/6$
Slant	$1/6$

Why's it called that?: Garnered the name in 1896 when a tenant farmholding was established here from a tiny tranche of the estates of the absurdly well-landed Lord Clinton. In the absence of any obvious cells or willow trees — the usual forebears of the name — one can only assume that his lordship whipped the appellation from Zeal Monachorum. If so, the place just means 'cell farm' which is rather uninviting really.

Where is it?: Not anywhere discernible.

Where exactly?: OS Landranger Map 191: SS4810 (fig. 1).

No, where *exactly*?: Top left-hand corner of the map, next to the unmarked Zeal Plantations, a wood shown with laudable accuracy by the OS as coniferous to the north and non-coniferous to the south, like the people.

Population: 3. Some chickens. Non-bipeds include two dogs (Milly and Molly; don't ask after their sister Mandy — it upsets them) and a handful of tenant cows.

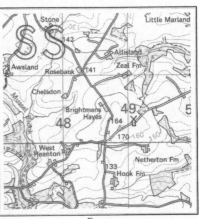

Fig. 1.

Getting there: March breezily out of King's Nympton station, tipping the goodly factotum a sovereign with the air of a person who can afford it. Breathe in lungfuls of nutritious Devonian air and head right along the A377, first right over the River Taw and on to Ashreigney, Riddlecombe and through Dolton. Make a

Fig. 2.

break for the River Torridge, a right at the A386 and first left towards Petrockstowe. Just before you get there, crane right, then right again – through Heanton Barton, a place named after itself – past the ruined windmill, then right, and Zeal Farm (figs 2 & 2a) is on your right.

What's there?: A stone-built house (built of stones in 1896 although not necessarily of 1,896 stones, though that would have been clever), four sheds (one of which was ye olde farmhouse made out of finest cob in the days befar any

of this new-fangled stone-building came into being and when the sighting of UFOs was still a seldom thing – didn't have time for them then, you see, coz we waz workin' that hard, still we

Fig. 2a.

dunna complain, not never, or you'd lose your job, see, and

that'd be that), a stables, a pigsty, 27 acres of grass, a lane, a well (capped, like a tooth), and a round-house which is square, held together by a tree, and in no little desuetude.

Things to do: Garden. Look after chickens. Renovate things. Develop an accent.

THINGS TO LOOK OUT FOR

Fig. 3.

Fig. 4.

Fig. 5.

☞ *Frog (imitation)* (fig. 3) – 3 POINTS.

Well (capped, like a boy scout, except that they no longer wear caps, apparently, which is why we no longer have an empire) (fig. 4) – 2 POINTS.

Lane (partial view — may contain ruts) (fig. 5) – 1 POINT. ✍

Nearest pub: The Laurels Inn (fig. 6), Petrockstowe, a village that is probably an anagram of something biting and satirical (like 'we stock toper', for example, or something even more bitingy and satiricaler).

Nearest public phone box: Next door to the Methodist Church, Petrockstowe, within stumbling and lurching distance of the pub.

Nearest body of water: The well, which comes from a spring, and a brook that runs across the grounds. Every day is different, you see.

Fig. 6.

What's furry?: Foxes, badgers, chickens, killer buzzards (see below).

What lives in the green bins?: The ancient restless souls of serfs, labourers, tied farmers, and chickens.

Role in Civil War: Dazzlingly close to the final conflict of any note. On the night of 16 February 1646, Lord Hopton and the remnants of Prince Charles' army were holed up in Torrington. Up the narrow streets, through the rainy murk, stormed the New Model Army. According to reports, the Royalists were done for even before their entire supply of gunpowder exploded, taking the roof off the church. Had it not been for the odd hill in between, you could have watched the whole thing from Zeal Farm, had it existed.

Claim to fame: Home to a brace of killer buzzards who made it into the national media by attacking local cyclists (admittedly, without actually killing any). Tragically, before they went on to host their own TV show (a late-night raptor-themed pop quiz – *Never Mind the Buzzards* – was already in pre-production), one of them was murdered. The other went underground, which is difficult for a buzzard and just shows to what a pass things had come.

Killer fact: The road that leads to Zeal was the main Tavistock to Bideford thoroughfare in the olden days when if you were turned off the land that was you finished, y'see, because you had nothing to offer but what your hands and body could labour at for ten hours a day under a broilin' sun with no food for a fortnight, the rent overdue, five hungry children abawlin' to be fed and (cont. overleaf)

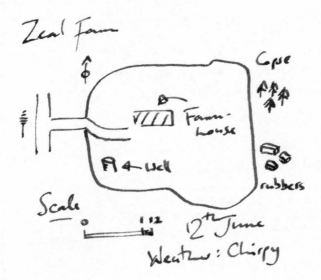

10

Zeal Farm (NE Devon)

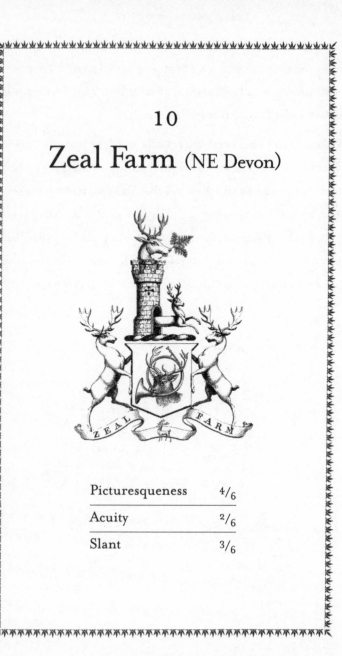

Picturesqueness	$4/6$
Acuity	$2/6$
Slant	$3/6$

Why's it called that?: It started life as Sayles – a name which first appears on maps in 1827 – but was soon corrupted by the Victorians, like so much else.

Where is it?: Not quite on Exmoor, not quite in the Brendon Hills, not quite in the Vale of Taunton. Imagine the life of St Antony of Padua, only represented in geographical form.

Where exactly?: OS Landranger Map 181: SS9922 (fig. 1).

No, where *exactly*?: Up a long Devonian hill which seems even longer if, say, your bicycle's bottom bracket has just sheared clean through at the foot of it.

Population: 8.

Getting there: From Tiverton Parkway station skip lightly but firmly towards Sampford Peverell but turn right just as your shadow darkens its door. Hop over the A361(T), follow your nose through Trumps (usually hearts in my experience) and turn right at the T-junction.

Fig. 1.

Describe an arc for a bit, taking a sharp right where a track leads off left towards Bampton, and Zeal Farm is on your right. For those whose lives are not brief, a longer route to the west takes you past Huntsham Castle and what is marked on the map as Weather Radar, which is either just a weather radar or an obtuse name for a hamlet. Mind you, this is the county that gave us Noble Hindrance, Little Pill and Snow Ball, so only a madman would rule anything out.

What's there?: A farmhouse, three stone barns, one non-stone barn, three sheds, 1,000 ewes and lambs, 30 cows and calves, 50-odd acres of arable land (barley, wheat, oats and beans – yum), some erstwhile farm cottages, and a bungalow across the road. For reasons which history has bathed in an impenetrable fog of unknowing and sinister mists of generational memory loss, the farmhouse has two bread ovens.

Things to do: Stride about. Bake things twice. Remark casually to an acquaintance that the word 'biscuit' means 'cooked twice' in French. Stare at the horizon, alone.

Fig. 2.

THINGS TO LOOK OUT FOR

☞ *'Installation 1: The Car Has Made Us Smaller'* (fig. 2) — 4 POINTS.

'Installation 2: Toadstools of Wrath' (fig. 3) — 2 POINTS.

'Installation 3: The Window of Hay' (fig. 4) — 1 POINT; 5 POINTS if you alert the artist to the fact that she has inadvertently used straw. ☜

Fig. 3.

Nearest pub: Now that The Barley Corn at Shillingford has gone to seed, the closest hostelry is the reputedly haunted Seahorse Inn at Bampton. The Staple Cross Inn at Staple Cross looks closer but, in tests, crows released from Zeal Farm reached the Seahorse considerably quicker, and were quite smug about it.

Fig. 4.

Nearest public phone box: At Shillingford, by what used to be The Barley Corn.

Nearest body of water: A tributary of the River Batherm courses gaily through the farm itself.

●●●

What's furry?: All manner of owls, ravens, falcons and red kites swoop down to view the red deer, roe deer and sika deer. It's a wonder any farming gets done at all.

What lives in the green bins?: Spilt silage, passing Victorians, overbaked bread.

Role in Civil War: The owner of the land at Zeal Farm was almost certainly a member of the neo-Roundhead clan

Fig. 5.

The Devon Clubmen, whose headquarters were in nearby Bampton. The existence of this group irked the Royalists, who duly marched down from Tiverton in 1645 and spent four days burning Bampton and its surrounds down to the ground. The Devon Clubmen unsuccessfully defended their property with pitchforks and cudgels — weapons that are effective enough when used in a dark alleyway but a bit rubbish in times of war.

Claim to fame: The Beast of Exmoor (see also Zabulon) has been sighted more than once on the farm, and is believed to have taken a sheep or two, though no ransom demands have ever been made. Big, jet-black and cat-like, The Beast is, in all probability, an escaped puma. Since it's the only one in these parts it's doubtless quite lonely, so if you have a puma at home you might consider taking it to Exmoor so that they can have tea together or something, or a natter over the carcass of some unwary farmhand.

Killer fact: Zeal Farm is purported to lie on the path of some ancient Druidic lanes (fig. 5). Ley lines plunder the land from east to west and curious miniature plateaux polka dot the plucky hill-top. Archaeologists from Tiverton Museum dig up these mystic platforms from time to time but find nothing. This is because Druids sneak in and move whatever is there before the archaeologists can get to it. I imagine.

16th June   Valentwal: Lustrous

ley line

Scale

1 LEY LINE

11

Zeal Farm (SE Devon)

Picturesqueness	4/6
Acuity	1/6
Slant	4/6

Why's it called that?: In common with many of the other Zeals that roam roguishly around the land, the name probably derives from 'sele' (or one of its plural forms, 'sealh'), the Old English for 'sallow tree', better known nowadays as the willow. Suggestions that the name is a corruption of Sophie Seal, the cheeky fish-eating amphibious mammal from *Dr Dolittle*, should be treated with the caution usually reserved for the shouted pronouncements of people wearing herring.

Where is it?: In the parish of Dunsford and Doddiscombsleigh, though disappointingly much closer to the former than the latter.

Where exactly?: OS Landranger Map 191: SX8189 (fig. 1).

No, where *exactly*?: On the patchwork quilt that is Devon, the farm can be found at the place where it tumbles over the side of the bed towards the inevitable bales of dust below.

Population: 2 + a pair of cats and an assortment of horses.

Fig. 1.

Getting there: At Exeter St David's station, a place so intrinsic that there are several senses in which it has always been there, head to your right up St David's Hill. Slide right at the Magdalen Street road contortion and down to a roundabout nothing like as intrinsic as the station but — in common with the Caspian Sea at night — rather too immense to be itself. Circumnavigate the greater part of this, eventually spiralling off at the B3212. Pass

Fig. 2.

under the railway bridge and proceed west as far as the hamlet of Reedy. Here you should effect a purposeful right turn, right again and then left at the crossroads. Zeal Farm is immediately to your left, a blank canvas for your brilliant mind.

What's there?: A jolly old house, a 15th-century barn, a stable, eighteen acres of land. This, however, is a bit of a comedown. As recently as 1987, Zeal Farm (fig. 6) had a populace of a couple of dozen and 300 acres for them to wander about on. Alas, no more.

Things to do: Look at the horses; read the Dunsford and Doddiscombsleigh parish magazine; look at the horses again; memorise the small ads section of the Dunsford and Doddiscombsleigh parish magazine and have a friend test you on it.

THINGS TO LOOK OUT FOR

☞ *The head of a horse* (fig. 3) — 1 POINT; 4 POINTS if attached to the body of a horse.

A huge cob chimney (fig. 4) — 1 POINT; 2 POINTS if you can explain precisely what cob is and, more pressingly, why it is what it is.

Zeal Farm sign (fig. 2) — 1 POINT; 2 POINTS

Fig. 3.

if the sign speaks to you in the voice of a long-dead music hall entertainer. ☜

Nearest pub: The Royal Oak (fig. 5), Dunsford (quiz night Thursdays).

Fig. 4.

Nearest public phone box: Opposite St Mary's Church in Dunsford.

Nearest body of water: Reedy Brook, whose reedy brookiness runneth past the very gates of the farm.

What's furry?: Grouse, grouses, grice; horse, horses, hice.

What lives in the green bins?: Well-thumbed copies of the parish magazine. Spare cob.

Fig. 5.

Role in Civil War: A mildly curious onlooker as the nearby Fulford House withstood a ten-day siege by Roundheads in 1645. In the rough and tumble of warfare, a ten-day siege ranks as a bit of a half-hearted affair. Worse still, Fulford House wasn't even a bona fide castle and yet it still managed to hold off the attackers. It must be assumed that the Parliamentarians involved found it difficult to look themselves in the mirror for some time afterwards.

Claim to fame: The cob chimney is the most like itself for some distance, apparently.

Killer fact: The farmhouse has its own well. Admittedly, this is not so much a killer

Fig. 6.

•••

fact as one that might, at best, maim an unwary bystander. However, it behoves us to remember that killers themselves are often duller than the film industry would have us believe.

12

Zeal Farm (Somerset)

Picturesqueness	$^4/_6$
Acuity	$^2/_6$
Slant	$^6/_6$

Why's it called that?: 'Zeal' has been likened by some to the German 'Zeile' (line or row) while others go for the more prosaic 'Zellestoff' (cellulose). However, the owners of Zeal Farm believe that the name derives, rather less romantically, from the Old English 'seale' which they doggedly avow signifies 'the seat of the squire'. Their argument is strengthened by the fact that, as far as can be ascertained, the farm has never produced cellulose in large quantities, or in lines.

Where is it?: The farm bestraddles the border between Somerset and Devon like lateral moraine gone soft in a comfortable glaciated valley.

Where exactly?: OS Landranger Map 181: SS8530 (fig. 1).

No, where *exactly*?: On the southernmost reaches of Exmoor, at the point where it tumbles down contours of alarming propinquity. Bring skis.

Population: 2 + cat (sceptical but over-reliant on Nietzsche) + dog (mad but not barking).

Fig. 1.

Getting there: Extracting an impish smut from your eye, ride jauntily away from Minehead station — the first and last stop on Britain's longest preserved steam railway. With the sea breezes behind you, strike up left through town, preferably joining the A39 the second time you reach it. After a couple of miles of westward pedalling, take a left to Blackford at which point turn right for Luccombe. The Exford road just to the west of Luccombe hauls the traveller onto Exmoor. Curious little angular roads unite Exford with Withypool. Glide serenely past the latter's church and, just as you feel the village is at an end, turn left down a road that forms part of the Two Moors Way. At the end, turn left towards Hawkridge, resisting the temptation to visit same. Zeal Farm is on your right where the hill drops away like an unfinished

What's there?: Zeal Farm is virtually a county in its own right, laying claim to 1,050 acres of land which, during the winter months, makes it twice the size of Wales. Over this vast dominion 250 cattle roam alongside 1,500 sheep. There is a farmhouse, firmly in Somerset, some barns, and a ruined circular wall that used to house a giant waterwheel that ran the thresher, chaff cutters, root cutters and sheep shears.

Things to do: Farm. Join the parish council (refreshments provided). Propose the establishment of Zealshire (agenda item no. 4).

THINGS TO LOOK OUT FOR

☞ *Waterwheel wall, with hole — (a design fault that cannot but have left the waterwheel somewhat hamstrung)* (fig. 2) — 2 POINTS.

A view, with hedge (fig. 3) — 1 POINT.

A different view, although to say that a view is different is to assert that we do not all see the same view differently anyway (fig. 4) — 1 POINT. ☜

Fig. 2.

Nearest pub: Technically, The London Inn at Molland, though it's over a hill or two and the road to it is wendy-windy. The Bridge at Dulverton is more accessible and, unlike a lot of pubs, is also available as a cross-stitch pattern kit (Country Needlecraft, £19.50).

Fig. 3.

Nearest public phone box: Hawkridge village, a good 750 yards away as the twenty pence pieces jingle.

Fig. 4.

Nearest body of water: A very large pond near the farmhouse. The size attests to the fact that, in days gone by, Zealshire (agenda item approved unanimously) was home to a bustling (and thirsty, it would seem) population.

What's furry?: Deer, foxes, badgers, sparrows, hen harriers (lock up your hens).

What lives in the green bins?: Minutes of past meetings of the Hawkridge parish council; remnants of harried hens; any other business.

Role in Civil War: A good deal of unpleasantness occurred during the war in nearby towns such as Barnstaple and Taunton. The parish of Hawkridge, however, avoided first-hand experience of violence by taking the expedient steps of tucking itself away in a little-visited part of Exmoor; not getting in anyone's way; and not declaring itself an anarcho-syndicalist commune committed to the overthrow of society and/or the re-introduction of Henry IV. Wisdom, as they say, wears no gimlet.

Claim to fame: Nearby Dulverton is the setting for a good deal of R.D. Blackmore's *Lorna Doone* so you can rest assured that those mad, bad and dangerous to know Doone types were swarming all over Zeal Farm at some time or other, and doubtless up to no good as they did so. It's a marvel the farm itself hasn't been stolen and dragged off to their lair to be killed and eaten with neeps and tatties and such like.

Killer fact: Three thousand years ago, inhabitants of Zeal Farm could cross the River Barle only at Tarr Steps, a clapper bridge built by the devil as a result of a bet with a local giant. This may seem unfortunate but it was the only way large-scale engineering projects ever got done in those days.

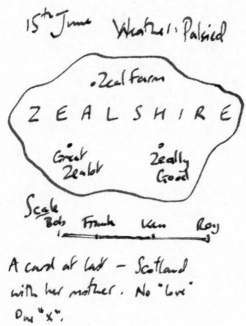

15th June   Weather: Palsied

Zeal Farm

ZEALSHIRE

Great Zealot   Zeally Good

Scale   Bob   Frank   Ken   Roy

A card at last — Scotland with her mother. No "love"
One "x".

13

Zeal Monachorum

Picturesqueness	$^4/_6$
Acuity	$^2/_6$
Slant	$^5/_6$

Why's it called that?: Zeal Monachorum means 'Cell of the Monks' and nothing else. There was some funny business over the name in the 11th century, of course, but that's only to be expected. It had all started so well too – writing in 967, King Eadgar referred to the place, quite rightly, as Zeal Monachorum. However, he also developed an understandable enthusiasm for the moniker Lesmanoac. Saxon cartographers got wind of this and before you could say 'let's stick an æ in that somewhere' had started tinkering with the plot, first by referring to the place as Mockenfield; then setting it in 23rd-century Canada with Munckton; before losing it altogether – deliberately, I expect, by tossing

Fig. 1.

it down the back of a motte – with Monks Nymet, the suffix being a reference to the unkempt woodland thereabouts. Mercifully, the eternally misunderstood King Canute (that curious affair on the beach was intended to demonstrate to his fawning advisors that he *wasn't* actually God, a difficulty not many of us will ever have to overcome) put an end to the madness by restoring the village's original name and handing the manor over to the monks at Buckfast Abbey.

Where is it?: Just like the rest of Devon, it's on the side of a hill.

Where exactly?: OS Landranger Map 191: SS7204 (fig. 1).

No, where *exactly*?: On the side of a particular hill.

Population: 394, down from 650 in 1850. No one knows where the missing 256 are hiding.

Getting there: Contrary to legend, Morchard Road station is at Down St Mary and actually abuts the A377 rather than the Morchard Road itself, but then precision has always

Fig. 2.

been an over-rated virtue. Anyhow, a mere left, right, through, swing, on and left and the village is found (fig. 2). However, those who prefer to blight their lives with complicated love affairs and the like might conceivably take the northern route through Nymphayes.

What's there?: A whole village, albeit one without a post office any more. It does have a church, a village hall and a pub-cum-conference centre though, so mustn't grumble.

Things to do: Ask passers-by if they have any stamps.

Attend conferences. Ask passers-by if they have any passport application forms. Bewail the fact that 'More Tea, Vicar? — A Mixed Exhibition of Domestic Place Settings' has come and gone. Ask passers-by if they can cash your pension.

THINGS TO LOOK OUT FOR

Fig. 3.

☞ *Cell of the Monks sign (peeling emulsion on plywood)* (fig. 3) — 1 POINT.

The notice board (mixed media) (fig. 6) — 2 POINTS.

The Queen's bench (wood on wood) (fig. 5) — 1 POINT. ✑

Nearest pub: At the bottom of the village, what was Waie Farm is the now literally entrancing Waie Inn (fig. 4). Finding the way in would be a whole lot simpler if the pub had its name on it. However, perhaps the owners should be applauded for setting a small challenge in a society where so much comes too easily. Just look for a building too big to be a house, too small to be the seat of government of a former Soviet satellite state, but just the right size to be a conference centre with its own skittle alleys.

Fig. 4.

Fig. 5.

Nearest public phone box: In the very heart of the village, where you might expect the village hall to be. However, if this were the village hall, wedding receptions would be very cramped affairs indeed (albeit that it does come equipped with its own telephone which would be useful for ringing for a taxi afterwards).

Nearest body of water: The River Yeo (pronounced as in 'yo', the Spanish word for 'I' – are not all rivers reflections of ourselves?) laps the southern border like the tongue of an indolent lemur.

What's furry?: Blackcaps and willow warblers, though neither is likely to be found wearing a badge identifying themselves as such which makes it harder to know whether you've seen one or not.

What lives in the green bins?: Discarded identity badges; the wreckage of complicated love affairs.

Role in Civil War: The local burghers buried their Saxon font to save it from the attentions of Cromwell's cheery iconoclasts. It stayed buried for 300 years, which just shows how thorough people were in those days. To show there were no hard feelings, the goodly Puritans redecorated the chancel in the style of their choosing. Being folk way ahead of their time, the style they plumped for was 'distressed', a look achieved largely by the application of violence.

Fig. 6.

Claim to fame: Late Victorian novelist Maxwell Gray (aka Mary Gleed Tuttiett) was governess of the rectory at Zeal Monachorum when she wrote her two-volume *The Silence of Dean Maitland*. This was not, as one might imagine, the story of a boy who was unusually quiet, but the cod biography of a village, thought to be based on Calbourne in the Isle of Wight.

Killer fact: At 1,200 years old, the yew in the churchyard of St Peter the Apostle was sown in a land that was not yet called England. Meanwhile, each November, amateur rainfall readings are taken. 8th June Weather: None

14
Zeals

Picturesqueness	$^2/_6$
Acuity	$^2/_6$
Slant	$3/_6$

Why's it called that?: Probably derived from the Old English plural form 'sealas' ('sallies' in Wiltshire dialect), denoting the shrub variety of the sallow or willow tree. The village first imprinted itself on the national consciousness in 956 as Seale. Just over a century later the villagers were confusing the living daylights out of the Domesday Book compilers by spelling it both Sele and Sela. The township then embarked on a heroic philological odyssey, beginning with Seles (1176) and Celes (1264). By the 17th century the settlement was changing name more often than its inhabitants changed their jerkins: from Sayles (1629) to Zailes (1637) to Zeales (1665). If this were not enough, it's also variously been known as Sealles, Seeles, Sceles and Selys as vowel-shifts have ravaged the land. Visit now, while a zed prevails.

Where is it?: Snug in Wiltshire's unshaven folds.

Where exactly?: OS Landranger Map 183: ST7831 (fig. 1).

No, where *exactly*?: Just to the west of Mere, a village devoted to the art of self-deprecation.

Fig. 1.

Population: A recent census claims that 643 souls inhabit 281 houses, making Zeals the most populous zed in Britain. Heady stuff.

Getting there: Sidle north out of Gillingham station on the main road (B3081) through the town. Go straight over the roundabout and struggle on through Colesbrook to Milton on Stour, at which point hang a left before you get to the church. Follow the road round to the right and onwards, turning neither to the left nor to the right, even though the right seems like it's straight ahead. It is, but it's a dead end that stops in a kind of barren nothingness just short of the A303(T). You will know that you have chosen the correct road by the fact that it cunningly burrows under the A303(T) and leads straight into Zeals.

What's there?: Houses. At least 281 of them. If you like your villages residential, then Zeals is for you. The only buildings that aren't houses are St Martin's Church, a school, and a garage-cum-post-office-cum-grocers. There's also an adventure playground, for the adventurous, and an airfield, for those with the means to travel back in time to World War II.

Things to do: Go to church. Go to school. Buy petrol-cum-stamps-cum-groceries. Venture. Travel through time.

THINGS TO LOOK OUT FOR

☞ *A birdhouse* (fig. 2) – 2 POINTS.

St Martin's Church (fig. 3) – 1 POINT; 2 POINTS if complete with vicar.

Control tower for the erstwhile Zeals airfield (fig. 4) – 2 POINTS; 3 POINTS if you're something of a controlling person yourself. ✐

Fig. 2.

Nearest pub: Look no further than the Bell and Crown, situated about where the ankle might be if the village were a licensed dental practitioner of about average height. Life in inner-city Zeals is tough and gritty, like a pavement,

Fig. 3.

and quaffers at the village hostelry should not be surprised to hear that it once had its fruit machine stolen. It is not known how much fruit was in the machine at the time of the theft, but if you are offered any in suspicious circumstances by men purporting to be genuine greengrocers, you should report the matter to the police.

Fig. 4.

Nearest public phone box: There's a serviceable one on New Road more or less opposite the Bell and Crown.

Nearest body of water: The River Stour runs cheekily just to the west of the village.

What's furry?: Foxes, grass verges, mould.

What lives in the green bins?: The assorted imponderabilia of residential life; the leftovers from the urban banquet.

Role in Civil War: Presumably the future Charles II slipped through Zeals one night on his way to or from being hidden in an upper room in the nearby Zeals House, and if he didn't he really ought to have done, if only for the sake of the tourist trade.

Claim to fame: Zeals Park Rangers (founded c. 1910) went the entire 1970–71 season in Division 3 of the Blackmore Vale League without losing a single match. We'll never see their like again.

Killer fact: A 1994 photograph of Zeals School, taken to celebrate its reprieve from closure, features a pupil named Zephyn.

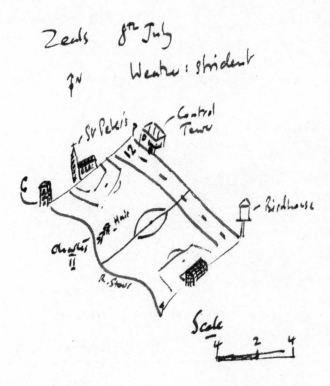

15

Zeals House

Picturesqueness	$4/6$
Acuity	$3/6$
Slant	$2/6$

Why's it called that?: Takes its name from nearby Zeals. It is a house.

Where is it?: Halfway between Zeals in the west and Mere in the exotic east.

Where exactly?: OS Landranger Map 183: ST7931 (fig. 1).

No, where *exactly*?: Bang right up against Lower Zeals.

Population: 7 + some miniature horses (although at first sight one might suspect that some ingenious trick of perspective is being played, it turns out that these horses really are just titchy, the bonsai of the equine world).

Fig. 1.

Getting there: From Zeals (14), strike out east along the main road until you hit a T-junction. Turn right under-neath the A303(T), and then immediately right again, as if you were going to join the A303(T) westbound traffic. Do not join the A303(T) westbound traffic. This would be a mistake, and one that cannot be rectified for some miles. You would feel upset and less of a person than you are now. The gated entrance to Zeals House is on the left of this slip road. It is guarded by two stone talbots, both of them fierce in a stone doggy sort of way though still unlikely to deter really determined burglars.

What's there?: A country house (fig. 2), built in 1304 but sadly biffed about by the Victorians; two lodge cottages; a boat house; an ice house; a three-storey apple store; a 17th-century orangery; a stable yard; a lake; two Georgian stable blocks; a clockhouse; a dovecote; and 60 acres of land. Loads, really.

Things to do: Breed miniature horses. Show them to people who like that sort of thing.

Fig. 2.

Fig. 3.

THINGS TO LOOK OUT FOR

☞ *Miniature horse (actual size)* (fig. 4) — 1 POINT.

Association football result stone (further evidence that Hindon's away record was once second to none) (fig. 5) — 1 POINT.

The lake (fig. 3) — 1 POINT. ☜

Fig. 4.

Nearest pub: The humble Butt of Sherry in Mere.

Nearest public phone box: In Mere's Church Street, a small street named after a minor church with nothing to recommend it particularly.

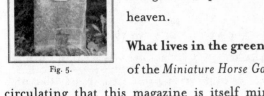

Fig. 5.

Nearest body of water: A lake in the grounds wherein live malignant carp.

What's furry?: Miniature horses, malignant carp. Not a match made in heaven.

What lives in the green bins?: Copies of the *Miniature Horse Gazette*. Rumours circulating that this magazine is itself miniature (being printed on paper not more than half an inch across) have long since been discounted, yet persist to this day.

Role in Civil War: The house is civilwartastic. A former owner, Hugh Grove, was beheaded for taking part in the Royalist uprising at South Molton in 1665. Also, the future Charles II was hidden in an upper room (fig. 6) for the night after fleeing from the calamitous Battle of Worcester in September 1651. Although of little consolation to Charles, who was to spend the next six weeks variously hiding in oaks and dressing as a serving maid en route to France, the battle at least brought an end to the violence in England, albeit temporarily.

Fig. 6.

Claim to fame: The ancient pile, which stayed in the same family from 1452 to 1968, is haunted by a young woman dressed in grey. The ghost is presumed to be that of a daughter of the house who eloped with a servant in 1876 and is believed to have been murdered in the grounds by same. There's a moral there somewhere.

Killer fact: Home to the British Miniature Horse Society, which holds its annual show in the grounds every August. Bring your own bunting.

8ᵗʰ July - afternoon

Weather : The same

a big house

COUGH

a little hoarse

16
Zeals Knoll

Picturesqueness	5/6
Acuity	2/6
Slant	5/6

Why's it called that?: It takes its name from nearby Zeals. It is a knoll.

Where is it?: A bit more to the west of Mere than you might imagine, assuming you're not accustomed to stretching your imagination all that much. The completely unhinged, on the other hand, should rein in their unfettered horizonless visions to about a couple of miles.

Where exactly?: OS Landranger Map 183: ST7933 (fig. 1).

No, where *exactly*?: Just north of the rather Eeyore-sounding Nor Wood.

Population: 0.

Getting there: From Zeals House (15), hang a right and right again and up the B3092 to the clock tower at Mere and I'll direct you from there ... Right, go back west along the same road you came in on — a bit annoying,

Fig. 1.

I know, but better safe than sorry, better the devil you know, a bird in the hand is worth two in the knoll etc. etc. — and turn right up a track just after Hillside Close. Follow this up along and round a field to a bridge over the A303. Carry on for a few hundred yards and Zeals Knoll is just the other side of the field to your left. Alternatively, parachute down using a plane, a parachute and a keen eye for topography.

What's there?: A hill with some trees on it forming a knoll, though some might argue that it's better described as a coppice. However, some people will argue about anything. They do it for the oxygen of publicity, a substance best kept under lock and key at a secret location. You, on the other hand, are Rationality herself and would never dream of basing your opinions on ignorance, a range of untested prejudices and wholesale bigotry.

Fig. 2.

Things to do: Identify species of tree. Hug duly identified species of tree. Remove splinters.

THINGS TO LOOK OUT FOR

Fig. 3.

☞ *Pre-knoll bushes* (fig. 2) — 1 POINT; 2 POINTS if they are burning without being consumed.

Unidentified farm machinery (fig. 3) — 2 POINTS; 3 POINTS if alien beings are seen emerging from it and taking over the world.

Mysteriously blank notice board (fig. 4) — 2 POINTS; 1 POINT if sullied by a notice of any kind. ✒

Nearest pub: The Butt of Sherry, in Mere, really not the exceptional village everyone says it is.

Nearest public phone box: In Mere, beside the George Inn which, although venerable, is really only one of hundreds of such pubs around the country that are just as nice.

Fig. 4.

Nearest body of water: The lake at Zeals House (carp, ghosts, tiny manure).

What's furry?: Flora and fauna for whom a wood (fig. 5) spells home — namely, the woodpigeon, woodcock, woodlark, woodpecker, wood warbler, woodhouse, woodlouse, wood grouse, woodworm, wood hyacinth, wood sorrel, woodbine, woodruff, wood nymph, wood.

Fig. 5.

What lives in the green bins?: Wood pulp.

Role in Civil War: Not a single drop of blood was shed on the knoll. Any soldier wounded there just kept it in until he was safely down the hill a bit.

Claim to fame: Part of the mighty Zeals empire made up originally of two medieval manors – Zeals Aylesbury and Zeals Clevedon. Admittedly, this isn't much to write home about but, historically, knolls have eschewed fame which they regard as tawdry and, like mulch, beneath them.

Killer fact: Knolls have been known to travel over 500 miles without landing.

8th July – evening
Weather: Testy

17
Zeaston

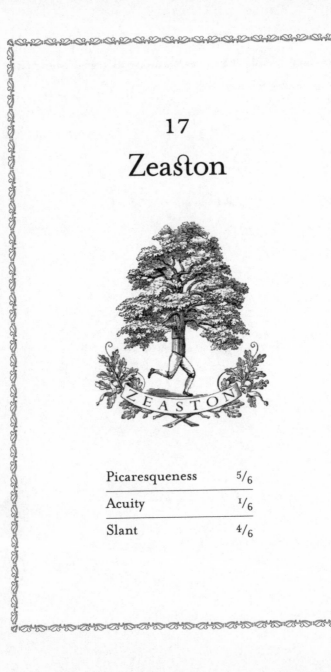

Picaresqueness	$5/6$
Acuity	$1/6$
Slant	$4/6$

Why's it called that?: Search me. Named after a ton of zeas, possibly, though more likely to have culled its suffix from the Saxon word meaning house or farm. The River Seaton, which sounds quite a lot like Zeaston, means 'twisting' in Cornish, and it would be nice to think that this former farm, with its one straight track off a road whose ruler-sharp lines would have made any Roman proud, shares much the same characteristics as that crinkly river just 25 miles to the west.

Where is it?: In the second layer of the chocolate box county that is Devon, next to the strawberry cream that nobody wants because it is, let us be frank, an offence to nature.

Where exactly?: OS Landranger Map 202: SX6858 (fig. 1).

No, where _exactly_?: A mile SSW of South Brent. This is more significant than it first seems because 200 years ago South Brent was not the byword for loucheness and picaresque dissembling that so peppers the conversation of today's misinformed neo-glitterati, but something quite different.

Fig. 1.

Population: 10.

Getting there: Nip out of Ivybridge station, swerve left onto the B3213 until it's just about ready to join the unfeasibly dull A38(T) where you take everyone by surprise by swinging dramatically to your right while simultaneously crossing a bridge over the trunk road. Take the first left and you'll find the entrance to Zeaston about half a mile along on your left.

What's there?: Notwithstanding the fact that the sign quite clearly says Zeaston Farm, there is no farm there any more. What is there is lots of converted farmness including a converted granary and a converted barn. There is also the original farmhouse (converted into a househouse), a couple of modern houses and a place where all the bins go.

Things to do: Convert things. Listen to the A38(T). Scream.

Fig. 2.

THINGS TO LOOK OUT FOR

Police aware ↰

Fig. 3.   Fig. 4.

☞ *Zeaston Farm sign* (fig. 2) – 1 POINT.

Abandoned car (fig. 3) – 3 POINTS.

Tree that looks not unlike a man, a man with a past at that (fig. 4) – 3 POINTS; 5 POINTS if seen speeding away in the abandoned car. ☜

Nearest pub: The Woodpecker Inn (fig. 5), just to the NE of Zeaston, with stunning views of the A38/A385 interchange.

Nearest public phone box: Crowder Park, South Brent. Ask for Florrie.

Nearest body of water: A mysterious unidentified brook just the other side of the A38 that appears to signal to pirates out at sea on stormy nights.

Fig. 5.

What's furry?: Cantaloupes, muffins (may cause hazardous road conditions in winter).

What lives in the green bins?: Farmhouses, granaries, barns. Anything else seeking conversion.

Role in Civil War: None in the literal sense. It spent the first half of the 17th century slyly pretending to be part of France until the coast was clear. Meanwhile, all around it, the war raged. Thomas Fairfax's troops were forever trooping past, either out from Exeter or on their way back to besiege it. On the other hand, Plymouth was lucky enough to be besieged and attacked twice by the Cavaliers. On both occasions the Roundheads held firm, having adroitly built themselves a line of triangular forts outside the town. In the meantime, the navy, which had quickly allied itself with Parliament, was constantly shuttling back and forth around the coast and generally making life miserable for any shipping not entirely won over to the rebels' cause. It's a wonder the people of Zeaston ever got enough peace to carry on their sybarite life of farming, shaking hands and, when the occasion warranted it, swithering.

Claim to fame: If Zeaston had a church, its bells would doubtless peal in grim rejoicing at the fact that the hamlet is now home to nearly 0.3% of the nation's Wonnacott population. The surname is derived from the Welsh word for skirting-board, but then so much is nowadays.

Killer fact: The last person to farm at Zeaston was a woman who some locals think 'may have been Austrian'.

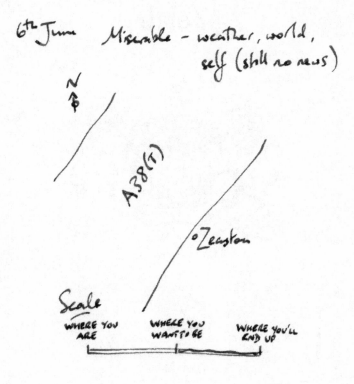

18
Zelah

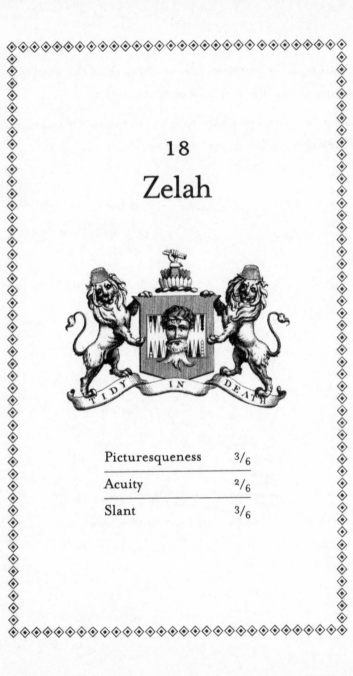

TIDY IN DEATH

Picturesqueness	3/6
Acuity	2/6
Slant	3/6

Why's it called that?: While some unreconstructed philologists continue to insist that Zelah is the offsping of a Saxon word for cell, it's much more likely to be a corruption of 'syghla', the Cornish for 'dry place'. Crucially, this latter theory is supported by the fact that the village is pronounced to rhyme with 'sealer' (a man employed by Celts to seal things in wax), rather than 'cellar' (a place employed by Saxons as a store for wine).

Where is it?: Just below Zelah Hill, a place employed by Celts to keep things high.

Where exactly?: OS Land-ranger Map 200/204: SW8151 (fig. 1).

No, where *exactly*?: Miles and miles from the nearest place of Saxon occupation.

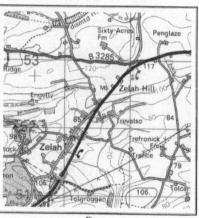

Fig. 1.

Population: 350-ish.

Getting there: Gone are the days when a trip to Zelah was the stuff of sci-fi novels and the ravings of fantasists. Now all a person has to do to get there is follow the instructions for Zelah Hill (20) and, rather than pushing on to the hill itself, simply stop at the place where it says

'... dip under the A30(T) and then right into Zelah' (fig. 2). Visitors should remember of course that they will still have to wear their trizon suit (including the geode head encaser), obtain travel clearance from the One Earth State Authorities in New London, and eat their daily xagron pill before they set out, as these are in short supply in the village ever since the Gronoths blockaded Star Corridor 4.

Fig. 2.

What's there?: A pub, a telephone box, Sansigra House (Motto: 'We're gonna live forever and so far we're doing OK.').

Things to do: Drink, phone, live forever.

THINGS TO LOOK OUT FOR

☞ *Deeply hilarious sign working on many levels for a range of different audiences* (fig. 3) — 2 POINTS.

Unamused bas-relief woman (fig. 5) — 3 POINTS.

Fig. 3.

Church hall, now defunct, beyond caring (fig. 6) — 1 POINT. ☜

Nearest pub: The Hawkins Arms (fig. 4), one-time watering hole of Tommy Cooper and purveyors of local ale Old Zelah Mist.

Nearest public phone box: Compensating to some degree for the deficiency of public spaces in the village, the phone box is one of the most desirable in the country. Furthermore, calls can be made in relative peace and quiet now that the A30 runs to the east of the village rather than straight through it.

Fig. 4.

Nearest body of water: The stream that gurgles forth at Zelah is an example to us all. From its inauspicious birth by the side of the ubiquitous A30 it swells to form the River Allen, becomes wide enough in its Truro River incarnation to permit sailing vessels, and blossoms into uncommon beauty as the River Fal before finally finding fame as Carrick Roads, one of the largest natural harbours

Fig. 5.

in the world. Too many people nowadays are born by the side of the A30 and think that good enough reason to give up hope when, by simply yielding to gravity and taking the path of least resistance, they could with time become an enormously capacious anchorage with ferries on (summer only).

Fig. 6.

What's furry?: Bitterns, woodcocks and weasels, all living in unexpected harmony.

What lives in the green bins?: The little egret's first breath; the basso profundo of diverted traffic.

Role in Civil War: The last remnants of the Royalist forces laid down their arms just down the road at Tresillian Bridge on 12 March 1646, signalling the end of the war, give or take the odd futile pocket of resistance.

Claim to fame: Steve Hallett, the former British Open Backgammon Champion, is a Zelah man. He now lives in quiet seclusion away from the trappings of vapid celebrity but, it is said, still within ear-shot of that insidious breaker of lesser men, the backgammoneer's dice shaker.

Killer fact: The village is officially dying. Just fifteen years ago it boasted two chapels, a Working Men's Club, a Women's Institute, a church hall, annual sports days and a summer fête. Today it has a pub, the last remnants of Royalist forces, and a beer so named because the brewers couldn't get it to clear.

19
Zelah Farm

Picturesqueness	3/6
Acuity	2/6
Slant	3/6

Why's it called that?: There's some irony going on here, or perhaps it's a bitter joke. Zelah Farm has a spring from which flows a stream down to the Helford River. Zelah, like its namesakes in the county, comes from the Cornish for 'dry place'.

Where is it?: Closer to beauty and ugliness than any of us.

Where exactly?: OS Land-ranger Map 203: SW6925 (fig. 1).

Fig. 1.

No, where *exactly*?: A duck's quack away from a seal sanctuary on the one side and the largest helicopter base in Europe on the other.

Population: 3.

Getting there: Penryn is a place that seems to be important for no particular reason and certainly no one from outside Cornwall has ever been there. If you yourself are not Cornish, you may have to explain to the guard that you wish to alight there. He is likely to be suspicious. Be polite but firm and, if necessary, make it clear that you are leaving the town at once on a journey that will take you many miles to the west. Assuming all goes well, be as good as your word and turn right onto Station Road, left, right, third right and follow your nose underneath the A39. This road will take you without further upset through Kergilliack, Lamanva, Ponjerevah and Constantine. At the village of Brill (in reality a bit of a disappointment), course left down to Gweek. Pass on through the soothing murk of

Fig. 2.

a tree-lined ceiling and, like Yeats, through the terrible novelty of light, stalk on, stalk on. Don't get too involved, though, or you're likely to miss the left turn to Zelah Farm.

What's there?: All that excretes is not a farm, as you'll soon discover, because, although this Zelah does an admirable impression of the cattle- and sheep-holding it once was, most of its land was sold off a few years ago to the herb farm next door. There are still 46 acres left, though, which is just about big enough to graze the three Hounds of Hades that live there now.

Things to do: Run away. These dogs — some sort of Alsatian/ sabre-tooth tiger cross-breed — would sooner tear you to pieces than attempt a simple crossword, even if every answer was either 'snarl' or 'grrr' and the prize was a lifetime's supply of warm raw flesh. To call them the quintessence of intimidation is to describe Lincolnshire as flattish.

THINGS TO LOOK OUT FOR

☞ *Blake's Hydram, a pump that cruelly finds itself almost permanently out of focus* (fig. 3) – 2 POINTS.

Name plate reached by handy steps (fig. 2) – 1 POINT.

Common comfrey, instantly identifiable by the inflorescences in the axils of the upper leaves (fig. 4) – 3 POINTS. ✑

Nearest pub: The Gweek Inn, Gweek (open all gweek, gweek in, gweek out, it's all Gweek to me etc. etc.).

Fig. 3.

Nearest public phone box: By the public viewing gallery-cum-café at Royal Naval Air Station Culdrose.

Fig. 4.

Nearest body of water: The spring phuts forth very near what used to be the farmhouse.

What's furry?: Woodpeckers, bullfinches, a barn owl, and anything else that can outrun the vicious wolf-beasts. Is it any accident that 'to dog' means to afflict?

What lives in the green bins?: Fur, feathers, bones, neighbours.

Role in Civil War: In 1648 there were Royalist uprisings breaking out around Zelah Farm more often than the Mayor of Helston slept through the night. Even so, with a bit of help from regular forces up from Penzance, he was generally able to give the insurgents a good rousting, thus saving England from the depredations of the Crown for ever, which in 17th-century terms meant until 1660.

Fig. 5.

Claim to fame: The Blake's Hydram Self-Acting Pump can magically push water around without using any external power aside from that produced by the spring itself. It is thus able to pump water up to the former farm's outbuildings without draining the world's resources (if you don't count the water itself, that is), adding to global warming or puncturing the ozone layer. There is even a helpful self-acting notice board explaining all its intricacies. If only more of us became self-acting, there'd be no need for taps.

Killer fact: Extraneous bits of RNAS Culdrose (which, in the armed forces' long-standing habit of favouring tradition over logic, is also called His Majesty's Ship *Seahawk*) are scattered about the fields around Zelah Farm (fig. 5). Lights, masts, and bits of metal last employed to keep the Chinese at bay dot the landscape like the remains of an immense steel camel that has been exploded thousands of feet above the runways in a disastrous experiment whose details are still covered by the Official Secrets Act and known only to incumbent Prime Ministers and the one surviving test pilot.

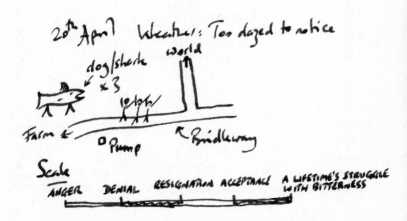

20
Zelah Hill

Picturesqueness	4/6
Acuity	4/6
Slant	4/6

Why's it called that?: Zelah, in common with the other Zelahs, is almost certainly derived from the Cornish word 'syghla' meaning 'dry place'. Hill is derived from the English word meaning 'naturally raised area of land'.

Where is it?: On a naturally raised area of dry land.

Where exactly?: OS Land-ranger Map 200/204: SW8152 (fig. 1).

Fig. 1.

No, where *exactly*?: Distance above sea-level: 360 feet — equivalent to the 110-metre hurdles, but with fewer hurdles.

Population: 11.

Getting there: Despite appearances to the contrary, Zelah Hill is a tiny bit closer to Truro than Newquay. If, however, you find yourself at Newquay station after, say, a visit to Zacry's Islands (2), arriving at Zelah Hill is simplicity itself. Just find some roads, make sure they pass through Gwills, St Newlyn East and Fiddlers Green, and travel upon them. If, on the other hand, you find yourself alone and unloved on a platform at Truro, at least the passage to Zelah Hill should make you a little more cheery. Take a right, assuming the weight of sadness has allowed you to make it to the front of the station; first right should see you over the railway, where you should effect another right at the end. The fourth left up a hill takes you onto the B3284 all the way to Shortlanesend. Slink right at the church and, after a bit, dip under the A30(T) and then right into Zelah. Joining the A30 at the top end of the village is likely to bring on all those feelings of dejection again, but it was still nice to be without them for a little while. Anyway, you're at Zelah Hill now so that's something.

What's there?: The A30(T). It's going to be 'moved down the hill' at some point because so many folk insist on crashing their cars at Zelah Hill and killing people.

Fig. 2.

Those few drivers who resist the temptation and make it out the other side invariably miss the smallholding (eight acres, two ponies), farm (sheep, cows), Zelah Hill Cottage (B&B, evening meal optional), and post-box (fig. 2).

Things to do: Interact with the postal system. Stay the night.

THINGS TO LOOK OUT FOR

☞ *Fence — redolent of the personal barriers we put up between ourselves and others* (fig. 3) — 2 POINTS.

Two Posts with Gap — there is always a distance between where one person ends and the next begins (fig. 4) — 3 POINTS.

Fig. 3.

View — we make the world smaller and then complain that we cannot get away from it all (fig. 5) — 1 POINT. ✍

Fig. 4.

Nearest pub: The 17th-century Hawkins Arms, home to the Zelah Hall of Fame.

Nearest public phone box: Also in Zelah, just a little further down the hill.

Nearest body of water: The Pastie Pool, a pond at the end of a field belonging to the smallholding (eight acres, two ponies).

What's furry?: Swallows, barn owls and buzzards — they share the same air space and yet would laugh if you told them they should employ air traffic controllers. What can we learn from them?

Fig. 5.

What lives in the green bins?: Fear, speed, nausea.

Role in Civil War: The last vestiges of Royalist resistance in Cornwall during the war proper were marshalled by a septuagenarian from Trerice, a house just a few short musket-ball volleys to the north-east. John Arundel found himself in command of Falmouth's Pendennis Castle and simultaneously besieged on the landward side and blockaded on the seaward. The horses starved first and were fed to the garrison. On 17 August 1646, after five months of living on dead horses and air, he succumbed to the inevitable and surrendered. However, the Roundheads were so impressed by the show that the 24 officers and 900 men had put up that they allowed them to march off to their homes with their standards flying and drums beating. Many of the men were so thankful to be out of the place they promptly died. Mind you, there was a lot of death in the 17th century so no one minded much.

Claim to fame: According to its owners, a 'really famous' disc jockey once spent the night at Zelah Hill Cottage. Such was his fame, in fact, that no one can quite remember who he was.

Killer fact: The Pastie Pool, aside from being at the end of a field belonging to the smallholding (eight acres, two ponies), is also right by the A30(T). The pond is home to some rare newts which means, happily, that the road cannot be enlarged at this point to give drivers more space in which to crash.

30th April   Weather: Ripping and/or topping

← Killer newt   Cars looking frightened →

Scale ___ yes ___ yes ___ No

21

Zell House Farm

Picturesqueness	$5/6$
Acuity	$3/6$
Slant	$2/6$

Why's it called that?: It isn't. Not any more, anyway. It's now called Zell Farmhouse (fig. 1), a name which cunningly

Fig. 1.

uses all the former names but in a different order, as if to confuse foreign spies and the like. To throw them off the scent even further, the farm is no longer a farm. Thanks to Zell Farmhouse, in the event of the outbreak of war, we're already winning.

Where is it?: Just a stone's throw from the Sandham Memorial Chapel at Burgh-clere, a monument to the dead of the Great War that took Sir Stanley Spencer six years to paint and which is considered one of the wonders of English art. Aside from

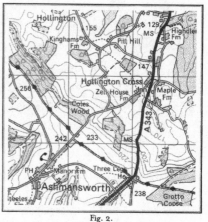

Fig. 2.

his genius with the brush, Spencer was known for his ability to throw stones well over two miles.

Where exactly?: OS Landranger Map 174: SU4358 (fig. 2).

No, where *exactly*?: Zell is to Hampshire as peckish is to esurient.

Population: 4 + 2 cats, 2 dogs, several chickens.

Getting there: From Newbury station, launch yourself right then second left and at the roundabout foist yourself upon the A343, a dull, drear but direct road. Sally through Wash Common, Great Pen Wood and Highclere, turning off right at the Yew Tree pub. Zell Farmhouse is but a few hundred yards further on.

What's there?: A 17th-century former farmhouse (fig. 3),

Fig. 3.

a former granary, a former open-fronted dairy, a former well, a former pigsty (now a chickensty), some former bees.

Things to do: Work out what things used to be before they became the things they are now. Establish, as far as is possible, what exactly it is they are now. Decide if the things they were were better than the things they became. Wander down the road for a few hundred yards sighing mournfully or rejoicing inwardly as appropriate. Keen recreational arborealists may wish to stop at this point and peer engagingly at Zell House Copse, a wood just to the south. Those who pity any sojourning amateur tree sleuths they may discover at that juncture should look to their own lives and see if their own contribution to the general good of humankind is any more substantial than that made by these gentle wood-loving folk.

THINGS TO LOOK OUT FOR

☞ *Granary — these are now quite rare due to their being torn down for use as the essential ingredient in granary bread* (fig. 4) – 1 POINT.

Fig. 4.

Barn — once confined to Barnstaple, where barns were invented (see also, staples), such buildings are now widespread (fig. 5) – 1 POINT.

Lawn (fig. 6) – 2 POINTS. ☜

Fig. 5.

Nearest pub: The Yew Tree, a hostelry that borders the Zell estate. You may find it expedient to win a large sum at Monte Carlo or similar before ordering.

Nearest public phone box: In the village of Ashmans-

Fig. 6.

worth, a good ten-minute hurtle if you need to call out the emergency services to arrest your inner *Id* or rescue a squirrel stuck up a tree.

Nearest body of water: A rain-water collection tank buried underneath the hardy perennials. If you find you have lost any rain-water recently, it may well have been collected here (bring proof of ownership and photographs).

What's furry?: Hares, chickens, barn owls, housemartins, mink (presumably on the run from a mink farm and no doubt carrying false papers).

What lives in the green bins?: Rare forgotten things like the novels of Rudyard Kipling, a neatly turned compliment, the correct usage of the word 'parboiled', and rickets.

Role in Civil War: Within furrowing distance of the first battle of Newbury (September 1643), much of which took place at Wash Common. Any closer and the confrontation would have had to be called the first battle of Zell House Farm, except that there was no second battle of Zell House Farm since the second battle of Newbury took place to the north, by Donnington Castle. Thus, $f = \frac{v \times t}{i}$ where f = the Future; v = Violence; t = Time; i = Infinite Number of Typing Monkeys.

Claim to fame: Max Bempreiksch, a Lithuanian Jew who escaped to Britain during World War II, grew honey on the farm and sold it under the name Zell Farm Bees. On quiet summer evenings, the extremely credulous can still pick out the ethereal buzz of ghostly bees, busy sowing honey seeds in fields that whisper of old Vilnius.

Killer fact: World War II was a busy time at Zell House Farm. Not only did Canadian soldiers dig wells here to practise for the Normandy landings (quite how useful they found this when pinned down on Juno Beach is not recorded) and plant the cherry tree which blossoms each year on the back lawn, but there was much excitement when a landmine exploded on the road to Ashmansworth, the impact of which made the west wall temporarily unsafe.

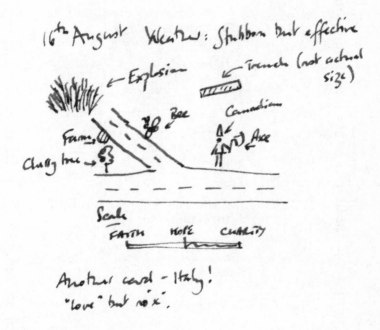

22
Zempson

WHAT PASSING BELLS FOR THESE WHO DIE AS CATTLE

Z · E · M · P · S · O · N

Picturesqueness	4/6
Acuity	2/6
Slant	3/6

Why's it called that?: Possibly a corruption of Seven Stones, possibly not.

Where is it?: Up a shale track (fig. 1). Shale, far from being the poor cousin of gravel, is actually a finely stratified rock. It

Fig. 1.

splits easily, like a headache, which makes it ideal for putting down and trampling on.

Where exactly?: OS Landranger Map 202: SX7162 (fig. 2).

No, where *exactly*?: If it had fingertips, it would have worn them out by now hanging on to the edge of Dartmoor. Its fingers would be bloodied tipless stumpy things with the power to make strong men retch and ladies faint away. For this reason they are permanently hidden away under gloves.

Population: 3.

Getting there: Take the South Devon Railway from Totnes to Buckfastleigh, refusing all offers of refreshment on the grounds that life itself is your food and drink. Skip, hungry and thirsty, over the A38(T) onto the B3380 and

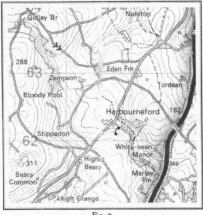

Fig. 2.

head leftwards. Sway to the right at the crossroads shortly after a farm and stagger right again when you reach the Zempson sign lost in the fastnesses of a hedge.

What's there?: A farm, two cottages, two barns, cattle, sheep, 177 acres of land.

Things to do: Stalk the Zempson sign. Imitate rusting farm equipment. Faint.

THINGS TO LOOK OUT FOR

☞ *Lost sign* (fig. 3) – 2 POINTS.

Improbably haunted greenhouse (fig. 4) – 1 POINT.

Plastic can of no return (fig. 5) – 3 POINTS. ☜

Fig. 3.

Nearest pub: The Royal Oak at South Brent (fig. 6), though the Church House Inn at Rattery is barely a crow's feather further away.

Fig. 4.

Nearest public phone box: In Harbourneford, a memorable sprint away.

Nearest body of water: The rippling River Harbourne trundles through Zempson on its way to the English Riviera.

What's furry?: Buzzards — so many indeed that it's often hard to hear oneself think for the buzzing.

What lives in the green bins?: Nothing much, since there's no collection here as such. Zempsonians thus trudge daily to the recycling centre in Buckfastleigh laden with cans, bottles and unwanted Goya prints.

Fig. 5.

Role in Civil War: Someone from these parts would almost certainly have been present at the nearby Battle of Bovey Heath (1646) in which Cromwell mopped up the last traces of the Devonian Cavalier garrisons and captured 150 cattle into the bargain, though why cattle were fighting in the first place remains a mystery.

Claim to fame: Zempson boasts two claims to fame, and each of them vies to out-forlorn the other. The first story is one of a bailiff who was foully murdered on Rowden Hill

Fig. 6.

by one William Moreshead, 'an unreasonable fellow'. Wangling a pardon for the crime apparently cost William's father a small fortune which, even in those days, was quite big. Still, it beats having your son hanged, probably. The sorry episode is recounted in full in the Reverend C.J. Perry Keane's *Dean Prior*. The second woeful account tells of an old local woman who wandered off one day and deliberately drowned herself in two feet of water in a pond in Dean Wood.

Killer fact: In the early 1900s a tenant farmer at Zempson was discovered breaking in a horse and was consequently evicted. This is further proof, if it were needed, that zero tolerance policing in those days habitually strayed into negative figures.

6th June Weather: Troubling to pesky

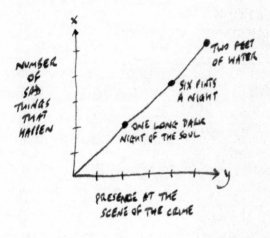

23

Zennor

MYTTIN DA, KATH

Picturesqueness	5/6
Acuity	1/6
Slant	4/6

Why's it called that?: The village is more correctly named Zennor Churchtown since this delineates it from the parish of Zennor. However, although remembering this does at least show local people that you have made an effort — something akin to learning the local words for 'hello', 'thank you' and 'hopscotch' before holidaying in Lithuania — do not feel under any pressure to use the full name more than you would your own during your stay in the community. Zennor is the modern spelling of Senar, a name given in honour of St Senara.

Fig. 1.

Where is it?: In exactly the right place for an experimental writers' commune.

Where exactly?: OS Landranger Map 203: SW4538 (fig. 1).

No, where *exactly*?: In exactly the right place for a quick getaway when, three months later, it all ends in tears.

Population: Roughly 100, with about 250 crammed inside the parish boundaries.

Getting there: The easiest way to get to Zennor (fig. 2) is to find yourself on Zennor Head (24) and work your way inland from there.

What's there?: All manner of thing. A café-cum-hostel made out of an old chapel, a church made out of an old church, a museum, two water wheels, an organic dairy farm, some cottages, a pub, a plague stone (in times of which, money going in or out of the village had to be dipped in the vinegar in the bowl of the stone in order to disinfect it — good times, those) and a Giant's Rock.

Fig. 2.

Things to do: Visit the Wayside Museum, so called because when it started in 1937, all the exhibits were displayed along the roadside. Zennor has more history per capita than anywhere in the known universe and is also quite pretty. Virginia Woolf, presumably without ever having visited everywhere else in order to check, still felt able to write: 'This is the loveliest place in the world.' D.H. Lawrence, meanwhile, got even more excitable: 'When I looked down at Zennor I knew it was the Promised Land and that a new heaven and a new earth would take place.' Writers, eh? It's all or nothing with that lot. Thank goodness, then, for Katherine Mansfield: 'It is not really a nice place. It is so full of high stones.'

THINGS TO LOOK OUT FOR

☞ *The Tinner of The Tinner's Arms, apparently armed with nothing more offensive than a pick-axe, although Trotsky, of course, was killed by something similar* (fig. 3) — 1 POINT.

Fig. 3.

Sundial, a handy reminder both that The Glory of the world Paseth, and that conventions in spelling and capitalisation Paseth too (fig. 4) — 2 POINTS.

The Mermaid of Zennor — wood carver's impression only; some features may differ from those as shown (fig. 5) — 3 POINTS. ☜

Nearest pub: The Tinner's Arms, opposite the church. Here D.H. Lawrence scribbled the last chapters of *Women in Love*.

Fig. 4.

Nearest public phone box: On the main road, a fraction to the east of the village.

Nearest body of water: The River With No Name makes its short journey from the Penwith hills to the sea via Zennor. However, that crashing sound you just heard was the collapse of the name's internal logic, for if the river is called The River With No Name, *ipso facto* it cannot be said to have no name. This is a lot for a small river to bear. Don't ask it questions.

What's furry?: Voles, shrews, badgers, organic cows.

What lives in the green bins?: Discarded plot lines, regional aphorisms.

Role in Civil War: A musket ball was found in a cottage roof but was, sadly, unlikely to have been fired in a bid to further the cause of either Rule by Parliament or the Divine Right of Kings since not much of that sort of behaviour went on around here.

Fig. 5.

Claim to fame: Zennor has been the cradle of so many notable happenings that nothing banal ever gets done here. First there's the whole mermaid business (see also Zennor Head); then John Davey, 'the last to possess any considerable Traditional Knowledge of the Cornish Language', dies in 1891 (he ended up talking to his cat, which is nice); 25 years later Lawrence has a stab at his utopian community; Virginia Woolf rents the same cottage a few years afterwards; Emperor Haile Selassie comes here to see out WWII before inadvertently becoming the focus of a religion; and Arnold Foster, first ever secretary of the League of Nations, also makes it his home. To make matters worse, his second wife is the widow of mountaineer George Mallory who died climbing Everest. Enough already.

Killer fact: The Giant of Zennor used to sit on the stone now called Giant's Rock. He no longer does so because he attempted a friendly pat on the head of a villager and, being a giant, fractured the poor chap's skull. Undone by remorse, the big man died of a broken heart. Something of an over-reaction, really, since his unintended victim probably recovered anyway. This is why giants have, as a rule, died out.

18th April Weather: Shining to apparent

Lady Chatterley's Larva

24

Zennor Head

Picturesqueness	6/6
Acuity	3/6
Slant	4/6

Why's it called that?: St Senara, who bestowed her name upon the village, was once plain old Princess Azenor. She married King Goello of Brittany and together they fell victim to the curse of the wicked stepmother story. If every tale of this nature were true, no single father in his right mind would marry again. Anyway, it seems that Azenor's father does so and, sure enough, when the princess becomes pregnant, her step-mother tells Goello that the child isn't his. Tsk. The would-be saint is condemned to death but her kind-hearted jailers save her by throwing her into the sea in a barrel. This is the sort of saving

Fig. 1.

that most of us could do without, but Azenor seemed to appreciate it nonetheless. So, there she is – a fugitive from injustice, pregnant, in a barrel, at the mercy of the sea. Sadly, that's all we've got time for this week.

Where is it?: More or less where it's been since it first started supporting farming communities in the early Bronze Age.

Where exactly?: OS Landranger Map 203: SW4439 (fig. 1).

No, where *exactly*?: Actually, a few feet south-east of its position in the early Bronze Age. As would you or I be after 4,000 years of exposure to the Atlantic.

Fig. 2.

Population: 0.

Getting there: Let's imagine for a moment that you're at Zennor Quoit (25) being exposed to 4,000 years of the Atlantic. Aside from the consequent crumbling of the ectoderm, it can also get quite lonely up there so you're probably none too unhappy about trekking down to Zennor Head for a chat with a chough. Start off by scything north-east along an initially wide path heading straight for a high stone wall that turns out to be part of a ruined house. Turn left when you reach same and follow the path down to the road. Turn left again and either wander into the village, effecting a right just after the phone box and then slipping out to Zennor Head on the path just behind the

Tinner's Arms (fig. 3), or follow the footpath down to Tregerthen and across to the pub before having a crack at the Head.

Fig. 3.

What's there?: Killas rock — compressed sediments that a while back had somewhat traumatic dealings with molten granite; a zawn; a ridge; some adits (drainage tunnels from copper and tin mines); and a couple of tors. Actually, for a bit of headland it's done quite well.

Things to do: Listen for the Mermaid of Zennor. Compress sediment.

THINGS TO LOOK OUT FOR

Fig. 4.

☞ *A raw tor* (fig. 2) — 1 POINT.

A lone stone (fig. 4) — 2 POINTS.

Pendour Cove; on account of the mermaid, it mustn't be rhymed with anything (fig. 5) — 1 POINT. ✍

Nearest pub: The Tinner's Arms, the perfect place for reading the Zennor-based nightmare sequence in D.H. Lawrence's novel *Kangaroo*.

Nearest public phone box: Still just to the east of the village.

Nearest body of water: The self-refuting paradox that is The River With No Name truffles along the Head before

Fig. 5.

plunging into Pendour (or Mermaid's) Cove. The sea is more or less everywhere else.

What's furry?: Once upon a time, choughs — imagine a crow with a hangover — scrambled about the cliffs. Entirely driven away by bad people, a few pairs have since been reintroduced on this coastline but you'd still count yourself very choughed if you saw one. However, consolation is at hand in the form of the dazzling array of butterflies on the Head, including the Large Blue (large, blue). They flit above the headland in that strangely other-worldly manner that butterflies have, as if they're just happy to be here.

What lives in the green bins?: Spent cocoons, a tail's scales.

Role in Civil War: In February 1916, Lawrence and his German wife Frieda Von Richthofen (a relation of The Red Baron) moved in just up the coast. By October 1917 they were being given three days to leave Cornwall. The couple were in the habit of leaving their curtains open at night and the locals suspected they were signalling to German U-boats off Zennor Head. In a sense, this episode was Zennor's own Civil War, only in miniature and with fewer pike-staffs.

Claim to fame: Local lad Matthew Trewhella fell in love with a beautiful but mysterious young girl who sang like an angel. Inevitably, perhaps, she lured him out to Pendour Cove and they were never seen again. According to reports, the girl turned out to be a mermaid, which was a cunning move. Matthew is thought to have adapted well enough to sub-aqua life and the couple are said to have had several children. The girl can often be heard singing down in the cove so there's no reason to believe this story isn't entirely true.

Killer fact: Helen Dunmore's *Zennor in Darkness* won the Orange Prize for fiction. It's the story of Lawrence and Frieda and wartime and suspicion and love and betrayal and a girl called Clare. Just as in *The Heart of Darkness* the title's darkness is largely figurative, so fans of literal darkness are likely to be disappointed.

18th Aprl - afternoon   Weather: Disparaging

ZENNOR HEAD

GIANT'S ROCK

300'

DISTANCE BETWEEN A ROCK
AND A HALF-PLAICE

MERMAID

25

Zennor Quoît

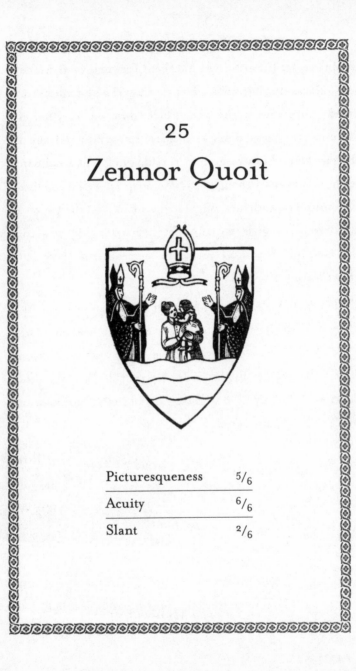

Picturesqueness	$5/6$
Acuity	$6/6$
Slant	$2/6$

Why's it called that?: An angel visits the pregnant Azenor — condemned to death by her own husband and adrift in a barrel somewhere off the Breton coast (a situation explained at Zennor Head — do keep up) — and she is delivered of a baby boy amid the waves. This unorthodox entry into the world doesn't hold little Budoc back any, and he becomes a bishop in Ireland (though not immediately, obviously). Meanwhile, Azenor's wicked stepmother confesses on her deathbed that her step-daughter's husband, King Goello, was the father of the child all along. Goello promptly calls his wife and son back from Ireland. On their way back to Brittany, they stop off at Cornwall to found a church and Senar — later Zennor — is born.

Fig. 1.

Fig. 2.

Azenor goes on to become St Senara, presumably attaining sainthood for not putting a meat-cleaver through her psychopathic yet gullible husband. A quoit, in the meantime, is the flat stone of a dolmen or, more ambitiously, the dolmen itself.

Where is it?: Legend has it that if you move the stones they will return here by themselves, so you can be pretty sure they'll be here when you turn up.

Where exactly?: OS Landranger Map 203: SW4638 (fig. 1).

No, where *exactly*?: Just where you might expect a burial chamber to be — in the midst of some peculiarly eerie downs that you wouldn't necessarily choose to get caught out on at night.

Population: 0. Some dead people.

Getting there: Leaving your meat-cleaver safely at home, turn right out of Penzance station, left onto the B3311, left at Amalebra, through Towednack, left again at the B3306 and the path is on your left after about a mile, marked by two stones (fig. 2). At the fork, take a left up to a ruined house. Turn sharp right and, all being well, after a bit you'll come upon the quoit.

What's there?: The largest quoit in Europe, probably dating from between 3000 and 4000 BC. The double capstone is partially collapsed but it still more or less forms a chamber with the five upright stones. The fact that it's still here is thanks to the vicar of Zennor, William Borlase, who in 1861 paid a local farmer five shillings not to break it up to build a cattle shelter. The cattle apparently tried to outbid the reverend, but even pooling their resources they couldn't raise more than four pieces of gorse and a teasel.

Things to do: If alone, remark: 'I've never seen anything quoit like it.' If in company, do not say this out loud, just allow yourself a wry chuckle. With any luck people will think you're enigmatic.

THINGS TO LOOK OUT FOR

☞ *View* (fig. 3) – 1 POINT.

Alternative view (fig. 4) – 1 POINT.

Lowering clouds (fig. 5) – 2 POINTS. ✍

Fig. 3.

Fig. 4.

Nearest pub: The Tinner's Arms, Zennor (*Women in Love*, *Kangaroo*, trouble with the censors).

Nearest public phone box: Clinging grimly onto the eastern edge of Zennor.

Nearest body of water: Rain, usually. Otherwise, The Nearest Body of Water With No Name, just to the west.

Fig. 5.

What's furry?: Grasshopper warblers and startled chiffchaffs blown up from the coves.

What lives in the green bins?: The past. We're always recycling the past.

Role in Civil War: One could idly speculate that some poor soldier toiling homeward from the latest bloody skirmish made it as far as the quoit and, with night already upon him and a storm coming in from the sea, he took refuge within. That night, his dreams filled with cannon, musketry and the death throes of his comrades, he resolved that he would lay down his weapon and become a poet. On awaking the next morning he would prove himself by writing a poem about the first thing he saw. As the new day dawned he opened his eyes and high up in the sky, through a gap in the rocks, he spied a chiffchaff. His celebrated poem, 'The Chiffchaff Meets the Riffraff', was only prevented from coming into being by the fact that he mistook the bird for a willow warbler. Finding nothing to rhyme with it, he retrieved his weapon, trudged back to the war, and was cold in his grave before the sun went down. Tragic really.

Claim to fame: It *is* the largest quoit in Europe. So few other places can claim that.

Killer fact: Local poet Henry Quick (1792–1857) lived all his life in Zennor and no doubt took inspiration from the quoit. A fragment of his poetry is reproduced here from his 'The Life and Progress of Henry Quick, of Zennor, Written by himself': 'In Zennor Parish I was born/ On Cornwall Coast remember/My birthday was in ninety two/The fourth of December.' You'll not be surprised to learn that he made the 1896 edition of the *Dictionary of National Biography*.

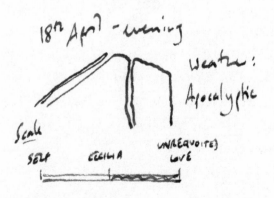

26
Zig Zag Hill

Picturesqueness	$^6/_6$
Acuity	$^4/_6$
Slant	$^6/_6$

Why's it called that?: It is a hill, and verily the road upon it ziggeth and zaggeth, repeatedly. One of the few noble Zs not to begin life as an S.

Where is it?: A little to the south-east of the self-consciously historic town of Shaftesbury.

Where exactly?: OS Landranger Map 184: ST8920 (fig. 1).

No, where *exactly*?: Nowhere exactly.

Population: Nada. Zilch. Nowt. Don't bother opening a hairdressing salon here, for your scissors will remain idle and your coffee, which tastes of the diseased parts of acorns, will grow cold.

Fig. 1.

Getting there: Stride purposefully out of Gillingham station in Dorset. Under no circumstances should you stride out of Gillingham station in Kent. Not only is the latter Gillingham pronounced differently, it is in a profoundly distinct part of the country and, on the Day

Fig. 2.

of Reckoning, the degree of purpose with which you stride from it will matter not one whit. Lurch to your right along the B3081 all the way to Shaftesbury. Stop lurching and haul yourself up through same, humming the music from the Hovis advert if you really must, and pop out the other side at a dull but functional roundabout wherein the A350 and the A30 converge. Endure the latter briefly before sidling off to the right along the B3081 and through Cann Common. Before you know it you'll be tearing up Zig Zag Hill (fig. 2) like an arrow through clotted cream.

What's there?: A hill, a road, some trees, some fields, some road signs, a fence, a view, a carpark.

Things to do: Look at the view. Practise parking. Open a hairdressing salon.

Fig. 3.

THINGS TO LOOK OUT FOR

☞ *A zig* (fig. 4) – 1 POINT (must be spotted up-zag from the curve).

A zag (fig. 5) – 1 POINT (must be spotted down-zig from the bend).

A view (fig. 3) – 1 POINT (must be spotted). ☜

Nearest pub: The Half Moon, Lower Blandford Road, Royal Chase Roundabout, edge of Shaftesbury. Not exactly homely. You might want to consider finding the other half and going there instead.

Fig. 4.

Fig. 5.

Nearest public phone box: Cann Common, on the main road just a few short strides from Lower Barn Close. Handy post box and parish notice board attached (please leave for future visitors).

Nearest body of water: A slither of stream in East Melbury. To be honest, it's a bit dispiriting. Not recommended for those who never really got over their first love.

What's furry?: Linnets, wheatears, other small tricky-to-identify birds with wistful names.

What lives in the green bins?: Aspirations, mainly.

Role in Civil War: The road up Zig Zag Hill leads to Tollard Royal, from which fact you may draw your own conclusions.

Fig. 6.

Claim to fame: An all-too-rare example of a place named after a feature of the road that runs through it. Cf. the Wiltshire village of Chicane, the Kent hamlet of Bendy and the Berwickshire new town of Longawaitedtrafficcalmingmeasuresthoughsomelunatichasalreadyknockedover-oneofthebollards.

Killer fact: Despite having a population of 0, Zig Zag Hill still manages to bestride two counties: Dorset at the lower end and Wiltshire at the top. There is a no-man's-land of about 50 yards between the two county signs which would appear to belong to neither Dorset nor Wiltshire. Do not overstay your welcome here. The sense of bewildered countylessness engendered by this strip of land has been

known to push even the strongest of minds beyond the edge
of reason and up onto the hillock of uncertainty (fig. 6).

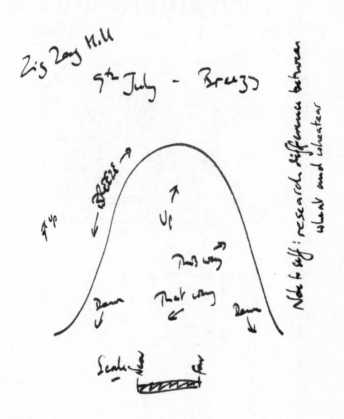

27

Zion Hill Farm (Hants)

Picturesqueness	$^2/_6$
Acuity	$^4/_6$
Slant	$^1/_6$

Why's it called that?: Not in Jerusalem, not on a hill, not a farm. Aside from that, the name accurately reflects this peculiarly dowdy few acres of Hampshire. OS maps erroneously refer to it as Zionshill Farm but the place was actually known as Sion Hill Farm until about twenty years ago when the Sion became Zion for reasons as apparent to the cows that grazed there as they are to us.

Where is it?: Just awry of Chandler's Ford.

Where exactly?: OS Landranger Map 185: SU4120 (fig. 1).

No, where *exactly*?: Strictly speaking, *il a disparu*. The story goes that, about a decade ago, the farmer simply walked off and left all his animals to the tender mercies of the developers. The story goes on that his wife died the very day they received the money from the sale of the farm,

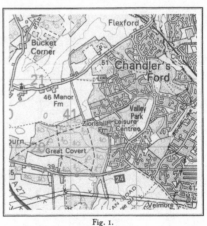

Fig. 1.

leaving the farmer without a farm and without a wife in one stroke. Expect this story to form the basis of a legend sometime in the future in which a strange curse on Zion Hill Farm accounts for the high incidence of madness among the inhabitants of the housing estate built upon it.

Getting there: Not for the faint-hearted since the farmhouse is now well hidden in the depths of a stupendously dull housing estate. From Eastleigh station, trot straight on up the partially pedestrianised Leigh Road which brings you out onto a very much busier Leigh Road. This dives under the M3 (roar roar) and where it ends you should plough more or less straight over and down Castle Lane, dismounting from your pony at the end like a good person, and leading it along the path to School Lane where your mount should bear left and then right at the roundabout onto Templars Way. Over the traffic lights you speed, right at the next roundabout onto Knightwood Road, left at the traffic lights down Sky's Wood Road, second left

Fig. 2.

up Blencowe Drive, right down Goldwire Drive, left between the bollards onto an unmade stretch of road and screech to a halt outside Zion Hill farmhouse. Easy-peasy. Completists might also wish to pay homage to Zion Hill Cottage, for which turn left down Castle Lane at the Templar's Way traffic lights and the cottage is on the right just before Misslebrook Lane.

What's there?: A farmhouse (fig. 2), a cottage, some fields, a housing estate.

Things to do: Research modern house-building techniques. Watch cars being washed (weekends only). Wonder how it is that we've come to this.

THINGS TO LOOK OUT FOR

Fig. 3.

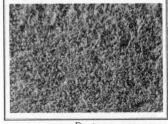
Fig. 4.

☞ *Barn-turned-garage, the ultimate triumph of the motorcar over animal foodstuffs* (fig. 3) – 1 POINT.

Bollard (must be this bollard) (fig. 5) – 1 POINT.

Hedge (must be this hedge) (fig. 4) – 1 POINT. ✐

Nearest pub: The Cleveland Bay, Valley Park, a stiff three-minute hike away. The name is not, as you might imagine, a tribute to a bay in Cleveland – the delightful Robin Hood's Bay springs immediately to mind – but a reference to a sort of horse, one presumably that came this

Fig. 5.

way *from* a bay in Cleveland, possibly ridden by Robin

Hood himself or, if not, by one of his lackeys — Will Scarlet perhaps, or that one whose name was ironic.

Nearest public phone box: Opposite The Cleveland Bay on George Perrett Way. Of course, sceptics claim that George Perrett's way was no better than anyone else's but don't mention that when you return to the bar or you'll never get served. They didn't much care for your 'bay in Cleveland' joke as it is.

Nearest body of water: Monk's Brook, a stream seldom used by monks nowadays, for any purpose, so presumably they would have no objections if you had a notion to holiday on its banks. The most popular times for this, of course, are Bank Holidays so if you do go then, do be prepared to queue.

What's furry?: Chamois leather, dice.

What lives in the green bins?: The distended reflection of your nose, in chrome.

Role in Civil War: No less a figure than Oliver Cromwell himself is reputed to have slept at the farmhouse, though why he did so is not entirely clear. One can only assume it was night time and he was tired.

Claim to fame: Er, no less a figure than Oliver Cromwell himself etc. etc.

Killer fact: The parish of North Baddesley, which includes Zion Hill Farm, is tripleted with Authie and Carpiquet, two small villages on the outskirts of Caen retaken by Canadian troops in World War II. Canadian soldiers practised for the Normandy landings at Zell House Farm (21). It is difficult to believe that this is a coincidence.

Weather: Fractious   15th August

Degrees of endearment

mild
~~vague~~ regard
Friendship   liking
admiration   ↑?
—— much fondness — oc? ——
keen   ↓?
Love   passionate
madly in love

28

Zion Hill Farm (N Yorks)

Picturesqueness	4/6
Acuity	4/6
Slant	1/6

Why's it called that?: A reference to the Hill of Zion, one of the two hills of ancient Jerusalem as pilfered by David from the Jebusites (2 Samuel 5:6–7). In common with the other Zion Hill Farm, it is not on a hill, or in Jerusalem, but at least it is a farm. Mercies, small, be thankful for them.

Where is it?: On the vast darkling plain that separates York from the North Yorkshire Moors.

Where exactly?: OS Landranger Map 100: SE5771 (fig. 1).

No, where *exactly*?: Under the mighty hill of Crayke, rescuer of maidens, slayer of dragons, chief examiner to the King's houmous.

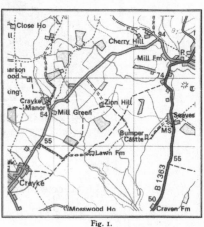

Fig. 1.

Population: 5 + one horse, two ponies and two dogs — a bumbling mongrel and a saluki, the only breed of dog not available in 3D.

Getting there: At York gawp, wide-eyed and foolish, at what was once the largest station building in Europe, before shepherding your thoughts, body and clothing left along Station Road, right into Station Avenue, through the city walls and over the River Ouse via Lendal Bridge. Hug the Museum Gardens, leaving them at last at Gillygate. Pitch left onto the B1363, here named Clarence Street, and shoot north across the flatnesses to Sutton-on-the-Forest. Turn left to press on through Huby and up into the fairytale hill settlement of Crayke, rescuer of maidens etc. Out, through and down the other side and a further mile will see you at journey's end.

Fig. 2.

What's there?: A dairy farm (fig. 2) of some 260 acres on which prowl 200 cows, the majority of whom are at a loss to know what to do with their allotted 1.3 acres other than chew it. Some of the more adventurous appear to have planted wheat and maize, a not inconsiderable feat for beasts with no opposable thumb. The rest is sheds, barns, houses, ponds and woodland.

Fig. 3.

Things to do: Chew things. Chew over things.

THINGS TO LOOK OUT FOR

Fig. 4.

Fig. 5.

☞ *A broken sign* (fig. 3) — 1 POINT.

A broken horse (fig. 4) — 2 POINTS.

Brown sticky pointy things (fig. 5) — 5 POINTS; 6 POINTS if you knew that the official collective nouns for such are 'a suppuration of pointy sticks' (winter and spring) and 'a lassitude of staves' (summer). In autumn, there is no collective noun. ✒

Nearest pub: The Durham Ox, Crayke (fig. 6). Quite posh.

The sort of place where men whose noble lineage is at best debatable leave behind shooting sticks encrusted with crests garnered at exclusive ski resorts whose slopes they have never darkened.

Fig. 6.

Nearest public phone box: At Crayke, on the other side of the road (unless you're on that side of the road, in which case you're right by it).

Nearest body of water: Two ponds in the farmhouse garden fester satisfyingly like the eyes of a condemned arsenical poisoner on the morning of his execution.

What's furry?: Badgers, foxes, ducks, curlews, woodpeckers. Sadly, the local kingfisher flew into a picture window, presumably by accident, and that was that.

Fig. 7.

What lives in the green bins?: The expectation that tomorrow will be a better day; toads.

Role in Civil War: Crayke Castle, a much-restored medieval pile whose territory once included Zion Hill Farm, declared for the King and was much damaged when besieged by the Roundheads. Evidence of combative unpleasantness extends to the farm itself in that several musket balls have been found there. The farm was already a couple of centuries old by the time the war kicked off, so doubtless the besiegers availed themselves of any crops or animals there. At the time, by a curious quirk of history, the farm was actually part of County Durham. In 685 AD, Crayke and the surrounding land was given to the Bishop of Durham by good King Ecgfrith. It didn't become part of the North Riding of York until 1844.

Claim to fame: Zion Hill's proverbial fifteen minutes actually lasted 10,080 by dint of its becoming the *Yorkshire Post*'s 'Farm of the Week' on account of the prodigiously tall maize that grew there one year. The expected recording contract never materialised, however, and the farm soon disappeared from the nation's radar screens.

Killer fact: A Neolithic axe-head mislaid (or perhaps buried as an artistic statement about the cruelty and senselessness of life) by some absent-minded (or tortured) Late Stone Age lumberjack (or installation artist) on a Tuesday in or around 3500 BC was unearthed on the farm a couple of years ago. Found to be difficult to sharpen and largely impractical in today's world of the combine harvester and the steam-driven comb, the axe-head has become a museum piece.

3rd August   Weather: Intimidating

Standard jokes from
the world of stick collectors

DO YOU
WANT A STICK?   NO
THANKS.   — YOU'VE BEEN
GIVING ME
STICK ALL
DAY.

← STICK
MEN →

29

Zion Place

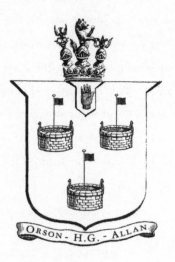

ORSON - H.G. - ALLAN

Picturesqueness	3/6
Acuity	5/6
Slant	1/6

Why's it called that?: Not only was Zion wrenched by David from the Jebusites, but the hill itself became synonymous with Jerusalem. The name also became synonymous with non-conformist chapels, so it's not a huge surprise to learn that the cottage – Collier House – that was the pub – The Jolly Colliers – was once the chapel.

Where is it?: It barely knows itself. Once firmly in Somerset, it moved to Avon and then just couldn't settle down. Currently starring in the unitary construct of Bath and North East Somerset, but might well have been claimed by Derbyshire by the time you get there so do check before you set off.

Where exactly?: OS Landranger Map 172: ST6459
(fig. 1).

No, where _exactly_?: 1.3 miles
south-east of Breach, 0.7
miles west of Mearns and an
eyebrow-raising 2.1 miles
south-south-west of The
Hawhaw.

Fig. 1.

Population: In so far as Zion Place no longer exists, it could be said not to have a population at all. Where it used to be there are roughly a score of hardy souls engaged in the hallowed country pursuits of living, breathing and recycling.

Getting there: Let's imagine, shall we, that your train has just blown in to Bath Spa. Wander insouciantly from the station and head into the setting sun. Continue out of town along the A367 which, as might be imagined from its

Fig. 2.

terrifying straightness, is indeed a Roman road. Take a right onto the B3115 at a sudden bendy bit where the Roman surveyors had evidently been a mite too

free and easy with the mead the night before. Follow this through Timsbury and out the other side like a cork from a champagne bottle. At the junction with the A39, hang a right then an immediate left down Cuckoo Lane which runs almost parallel with the A39. This leads you straight as a die to where Zion Place once was.

Fig. 3.

What's there?: Today's hearty seeker after truth will find Collier House (fig. 3), the Flower Barn, some former miners' cottages, three wells and a personal golf course.

Things to do: Look at the cottages. Look at the three wells. Put hands on hips and say: 'Well, well, well.' Laugh hysterically at own joke.

THINGS TO LOOK OUT FOR

Fig. 4.

Fig. 5.

☞ *Recycling bin* (fig. 4) – 1 POINT; 2 POINTS if filled entirely with spent Chianti bottles.

Cuckoo Lane sign (fig. 2) – 1 POINT; 0 POINTS if you knew that the road derived its name not from the nest-wetting bird but the nearby Cuckoo mine-working. Nobody likes a Clever Dick.

Zion Cottage sign (fig. 5) – 1 POINT. Grasp it and be thankful. ☜

Nearest pub: It used to have its own, of course, but The Jolly Colliers closed down in 1957. Nowadays The Star at High Littleton and the Hunter's Rest, just the other side of Clutton Hill, are equidistant. As you might expect, the Hunter's Rest has its own miniature railway (50p – half price on Wednesdays, just like the real thing), albeit that someone stole their train a couple of years ago. More a case of Shunter's Rest, really, but possibly best not to say this too loudly at the bar.

Nearest public phone box: Southern end of High Littleton.

Nearest body of water: The ponds at the suspiciously Jane Austen-sounding Greyfield House claim to be closest. More interestingly, there's a waterfall in Greyfield Woods. However, check out the 1884–87 OS map for the area and a spring is quite clearly marked just a few manly strides to the north-west of Zion Place. By the 1900 map, the spring is magically transformed into a coal shaft. What can it all mean? Soggy coal, I suppose.

What's furry?: Barn owls and tawny owls sit on the washing lines, staring obliquely into space and wondering what it is about themselves that anthropomorphises into wisdom.

What lives in the green bins?: Chianti bottles, plus-fours, Jebusites.

Role in Civil War: The land which was to become Zion Place almost certainly felt the thud of Fairfax's New Model Army as it marched triumphantly from Sherborne (besieged then blasted into oblivion) to Bristol (soon to be wrested from the lilywhite hands of Prince Rupert) in August 1645.

Claim to fame: Used to be in the midst of the Earl of Warwick's miniature mining empire with its own railway shuttling coal from various local pits. Greyfield House was owned by the boss of the coal mine; the cottages at Zion Place housed the oppressed and busily emphysemic miners.

Killer fact: Until everyone noticed that they could travel from Bristol to Bath rather more swiftly by heading south-east to where Bath is, rather than south, to where it isn't, Zion Place used to be on the main road between the two cities, with the pub acting as a coach house.

30

Zion's Hill

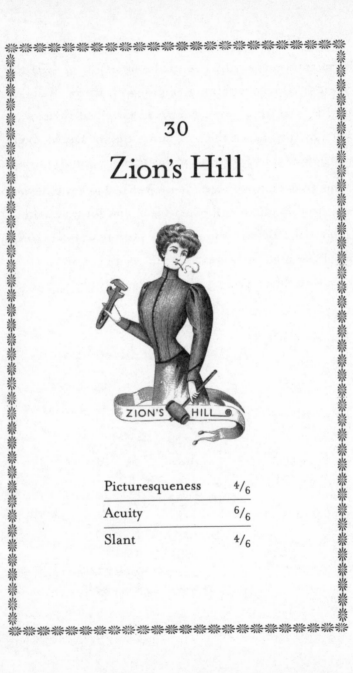

Picturesqueness	$4/6$
Acuity	$6/6$
Slant	$4/6$

Why's it called that?: In a very real sense, it isn't. At least, outside the village it's known as Golden Hill. Even recent OS maps proclaim it as such. However, arrive at Golden Hill and it becomes appallingly apparent that it's not Golden Hill at all but Zion's Hill, a name bequeathed it by its chapel. As with the other Zions, its name is derived from the Hill of Zion, a name synonymous with Jerusalem and, allegorically, heaven. Also sometimes known as Lewis Hill, but let's not get into that just now.

Where is it?: In Pembrokeshire, the county that brought you Britain's smallest city and Europe's deepest port.

Where exactly?: OS Land-ranger Map 157/158: SM9724 (fig. 1).

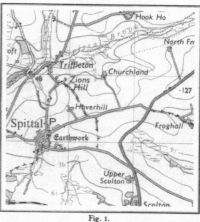

Fig. 1.

No, where _exactly_?: Half a mile north (and thus com-fortably out of range, even downwind) of Spittal.

Population: 57, give or take.

Getting there: Take the train to Clarbeston Road, a settlement now bigger than Clarbeston, which must seem ironic to those who remember the days when there was nothing there but a train station. Mind you, such people have probably got more pressing things to think about, like whether they're expected to reply to their telegram from the Queen. Turn left, then left over the bridge, take the first left, then left again at the crossroads. By rights, you should be back where you first started but this is Wales, magical realism's spiritual home, so you're actually doing very nicely. Trundle on to Spittal carrying, if at all possible, a badger who talks only of baby eels and lost time. At the church, take a right (or three lefts if you feel more comfortable with that) and slide through the chicane, following the sign to Golden Hill. In half a mile you shall be in Zion's Hill, though the badger will have mysteriously disappeared, only to turn up at some later point as a Mr Badger, the watch-mender, who will

Fig. 2.

serve you fried elvers whose bodies spell out your grandmother's name as they slide onto the plate.

What's there?: Zion's Hill Chapel; some cottages; a housing estate (not quite sure how this happened, but at least it's a nice posh one); an MOT testing station; an enormous graveyard. The dead of Zion's Hill far outnumber the living, as is only appropriate in a place named after heaven.

Things to do: Go to chapel. Hang around on the housing estate looking tough, but in a nice posh way. Examine graves. Think about own mortality for a bit. Wonder why no one in the village has ever heard of a Mr Badger, even though the unmistakeable smell of fried elvers still permeates the evening air like memories you're yet to have.

THINGS TO LOOK OUT FOR

☞ *The chapel, a place where low church simplicity and high art values come together in harmony* (fig. 2) – 1 POINT.

The garage, a place where quality waiting privacy and high parking values come together in harmony (fig. 3) – 2 POINTS.

Fig. 3.

The graveyard, a place where quality church simplicity and private parking values come together in harmony (fig. 4) – 3 POINTS. ☜

Fig. 4.

Nearest pub: Spittal's The Pump on the Green (fig. 5), a petrol station in a former life. Hence the pun.

Fig. 5.

Nearest public phone box: In Spittal, near the green —
preferable to it being in green near the spittle which is,
however, always a possibility.

Nearest body of water: Spittal Brook, inevitably, runs
through Zion's Hill at its northernmost extremity. It's the
sort of stream that gets bad poetry written about it by people
who think they are Rupert Brooke but rarely are.

What's furry?: Badgers, weasels, snowdrops and daffodils —
possibly the perfect combination.

What lives in the green bins?: Mysticism, ambiguity, some
corner of a foreign field.

Role in Civil War: The loquacious and randomly violent
Lord Carbery (he threatened to put the Mayor of Pembroke
into a barrel and roll him into the sea, like you do) and Sir
Henry Vaughan, the sheriff of Carmarthenshire, seized much
of solidly Parliamentarian Pembrokeshire for the King.

However, they were defeated by Rowland Laugharne, former page to Essex (the man, not the entire county, that would be ridiculous). Vaughan judiciously fled from Haverfordwest, a town just to the south of Zion's Hill. Four years later Laugharne was to switch sides, a practice that occurred with tedious regularity throughout the war (see Zabulon). One can only imagine that Lord Carbery was not best pleased when he heard.

Claim to fame: Zion's Hill is home to a significant proportion of the women members of the Institute of Plumbing and Heating Engineers. The hamlet is clearly the new London, only hipper, and with more feminised drainage.

Killer fact: Zion's Hill is the only one of the 41 zeds unrecognised by the Ordnance Survey *Gazetteer of Great Britain* which, like everyone else, has been taken in by the Golden Hill subterfuge. Heads will roll, of course.

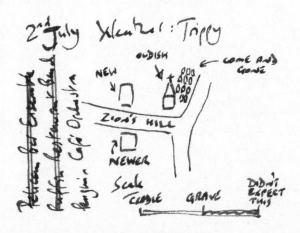

31

Zoar (Cornwall)

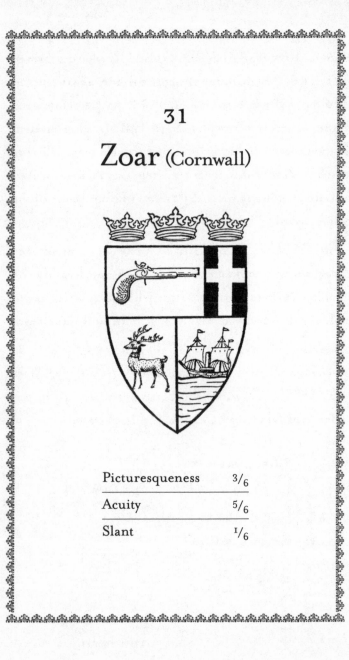

Picturesqueness	3/6
Acuity	5/6
Slant	1/6

Why's it called that?: In Genesis 19:22, Zoar is the town to which Lot (of wifely pillar of salt fame) escapes in order to avoid the wrath of God heaped on Sodom and Gomorrah (whose crime was not, as is generally assumed, licentiousness but social injustice, which is a sobering thought). Zoar (lit. 'small' in Hebrew) is thus usually associated with 'a place of refuge' and was the name of the erstwhile Methodist chapel built by local farmers in the days when piety was viewed as a virtue.

Where is it?: In the bit of the Lizard Peninsula that no one much knows about because anyone who takes the trouble to come anywhere near merely trolls down to Lizard Point where they find that the sea looks much like it does from any other point, before hurtling back up to Helston in time to mispronounce the Furry Dance.

Where exactly?: OS Landranger Map 204: SW7619 (fig. 1).

No, where *exactly*?: Under the shadow of Goonhilly listening station (fig. 2) so keep your voice down.

Population: 6.

Fig. 1.

Getting there: From Penmere station, manoeuvre yourself onto Boslowick Road and climb up out of Falmouth. At the very top, turn left to Maenporth and then right at the T-junction to Mawnan Smith. At the middle of the village — where, in the grocers, you might want to check the times of the Helford Ferry (it doesn't run at low tide) — turn left to Helford Passage, passing the gardens of Glendurgan. Once safely over to Helford, inch your way around the coast to Treath. Haul yourself up to Manaccan and drift along joyously tiny roads to Tregowris, Lesneague, the improbable-sounding Nambol, and Trevithian. Where the road joins the B3293, the deceptive cluster of notmuchness in front of you is Zoar.

Fig. 2.

Fig. 3.

What's there?: A Shetland pony stud, a dolmen, the site of a Methodist chapel, a scattering of dwellings, a petrol station, a coach hire firm. Dreamy.

Things to do: Speculate on what the Goonhilly people might be listening to from outer space. Worry for a bit. Seek refuge from the wrath of God.

THINGS TO LOOK OUT FOR

☞ *Where the Three Brothers of Grugith will be* (fig. 4) — 5 POINTS.

Where a coach is (fig. 3) — 3 POINTS.

Where the Methodist Chapel was (fig. 5) — 2 POINTS. ✐

Fig. 4.

Fig. 5.

Nearest pub: The Paris Hotel, Coverack. If you're booking accommodation in the French capital, this should probably come quite a way down your list because it's something of a hike to even the most far-flung Metro stations. Furthermore, it's more pub than hotel, and turns out to have been named after a liner that contrived to snag itself on The Manacles in 1899. In case you're still sceptical, they've a fine model of the *Paris* in a glass cabinet.

Nearest public phone box: At the foot of School Lane in coastally Coverack.

Nearest body of water: A borehole in the hamlet meets the aquatic needs of each and every hamleteer.

>•<

What's furry?: Adders, sparrowhawks, *Erica vagans*, Shetland ponies (given the existence of the Shetland Zoar, this is enough of a coincidence to make one feel a little uneasy).

What lives in the green bins?: *The Western Morning News, The West Briton, The Cornishman, Packet* (est. 1855, no 'the' required).

Role in Civil War: Unassuming though it might be today, an uprising once passed right through what is now Zoar. In 1648, during what is known as the Second Civil War (there were three if you're counting), Mullion was, as they rather charmingly put it, 'up'. Roughly 120 men marched out across Goonhilly Down, through Zoar and on to St Keverne before eventually looping right round to Mawgan. On their way they picked up another 300 foot soldiers and 40 more on horseback. At Mawgan, on 23 May, they encountered some Roundhead troops hastily assembled by the Mayor of Helston and were soon routed after retreating to an ancient earthwork called Gear. The 'Gear Rout', as it became known, ended with Royalists fleeing for their lives. Some apparently made it to the coast near St Keverne where, in despair, they joined hands and leapt into the sea.

Claim to fame: The Three Brothers of Grugith, a dolmen of indeterminate age, was apparently formed when St Keverne threw three stones at St Just for stealing his drinking cup. One can only conclude that in those days the criteria for canonisation weren't quite as exacting as they are today.

Killer fact: Ne'er-do-wells were hanged at the gibbet on the Zoar road at Traboe Cross. Parochial ghosts include a highwayman, a red deer and a sailing ship. Even for ghosts, that is quite eclectic.

Weather: Dribbly   21ˢᵗ April

MAWNAN SMITH

Scale DEFGABC#D

(SADDEST OF ALL)

32

Zoar (Devon)

Picturesqueness	5/6
Acuity	3/6
Slant	1/6

Why's it called that?: Even to those with a very keen ear, Zoar can still be confused with the Hebrew word for 'small'. The early-Victorian Zoar Chapel, which gave its name to the hamlet, was indeed quite small, but big in spirit, as were the people of those heady days when carrying an ailing bull on one's back for twenty miles of an afternoon was viewed as a respite from the daily grind. 'Lucky Dick Chuzzlewuck,' the local farm labourers would mutter enviously, 'the Master's sent him off to Okehampton with that ox what's sick.'

Where is it?: On the wild and blasted moor, sir, exposed like a man's sins on Judgement Day.

Where exactly?: OS Landranger Map 191/201: SX5280 (fig. 1).

Fig. 1.

No, where *exactly*?: Pitched between the sibling Dartmoor villages of Peter Tavy and Mary Tavy, and nowhere within striking distance of anywhere else.

Population: 7.

Getting there: Be the first person ever to travel to Gunnislake station, the end of a mysterious branch line that has probably never existed save in the minds of timetable planners. Breeze heartily along the A390 to Tavistock, making sure to nip off the main road from time to time to take the more direct but more taxing and therefore spiritually nourishing C-roads. At Tavistock, lurch off onto the B3357 and head east just out of town before throwing yourself left onto a minor road that wends its way up on to the moor and eventually arrives at Peter Tavy. Forge onwards through Cudlipptown and the next left takes you over a bridge and left onto a bridleway at Hillbridge Farm. This ploughs onerously through a surprising quantity of muddy puddles before popping out very close indeed to the unmarked terrace of cottages that is Zoar. Those employing penny farthings or similar may wish to avoid the mire by taking the long way round through Hilltown (on a hill of sorts, not

Fig. 2.

a town). If you arrive at Willsworthy, something's up.

What's there?: A terrace of four cottages (fig. 2), one of which used to be Zoar Chapel, the other three being extensions to same. Zoar Chapel was built in 1840 but was deconsecrated and converted into a cottage in 1904 when a nicer chapel down the road was opened, much to everyone's private glee, public glee being frowned on what with the Queen still warm in her grave.

Things to do: Zoar. What is it good for? Absolutely nothing. Say it again. Or rather don't, because you can go walking or riding or, better still, take up the popular local pursuit of rock counting.

THINGS TO LOOK OUT FOR

Fig. 3.   Fig. 4.

 Master Rock, Zoar Down (fig. 3) – 1 POINT. Non-locals should address it as Mister Rock.

The solitary lamp post (fig. 5) – 1 POINT. If it were in London, it would be art. Perhaps it is.

The four doors of Zoar (fig. 4) – 2 POINTS. They've won prizes for internal rhyming, you know. ✏

Nearest pub: The Elephant's Nest (fig. 6), Horndon (though to visit Zoar without also taking in the nearby Peter Tavy Inn is akin to travelling to Greenland and forgetting to bring home some green).

Nearest public phone box: In Horndon. Apparently, it is

Fig. 5.   Fig. 6.

at risk of imminent closure so you would be advised to make your calls brief.

Nearest body of water: The dammed pool up out on Zoar Down. The water running down from here turns an electricity-producing turbine in Mary Tavy, which is nice.

What's furry?: Badgers, woodpeckers, curious orange bulls, pheasants, manure.

What lives in the green bins?: Dusty communion wine bottles; sermon notes; kneelers.

Role in Civil War: In its time, Zoar has apparently been home to copper, silver and lead mines, the produce of all of which would have been useful to either side in the conflict. Okehampton was held for the King for the greater part of the war so one can only conclude that the Royalists derived most advantage from whatever was extracted here. The locals themselves narrowly avoided being caught up in a fracas up the road at Sourton Down when a small band of cavalry led by Major-General James Chudleigh ambushed Sir Ralph Hopton and killed about 60 Cavaliers. Not long afterwards, though, Chudleigh was captured and promptly changed sides, which doesn't seem to be quite in the spirit of things and must have been particularly irksome to the dead Cavaliers.

Claim to fame: Master (or Preacher's) Rock on Zoar Down was where recovering alcoholic Billy Bray preached to the mining masses before the first Zoar Chapel was erected.

Killer fact: The rocks scattered about Zoar Down were put there by pixies.

4th June   Weather: Hilarious, then sobering

Scale 0   Say it again

33

Zoar (Shetland)

Picturesqueness	4/6
Acuity	3/6
Sleet	5/6

Why's it called that?: Lit. 'small', which is fitting, I suppose, since it's not exactly a metropolis. The name was first given several centuries ago to a crofter's house, the ruins of which are still visible, if only to the naked eye. Furthermore, Shetland itself has spent some time as a zed. One of its Norse names was Hjaltland which, by the 16th century, had become Yetland. The printed form of the 'y' sound looked like our modern-day 'z' — hence Zetland. The name is still reflected in the fact that, rather stirringly, Zoar is in postcode district ZE2.

Fig. 1.

Where is it?: In the north-western bit of the mainland of Shetland. Not to be confused with two other houses in the Shetlands called Zoar — one at Wad-bister and the other, of course, on the Isle of Whalsay — neither of which merits an OS name-check.

Where exactly?: OS Landranger Map 3: HU2677 (fig. 1).

No, where *exactly*?: Beyond the end of nowhere, and then up a hill.

Population: 1 + Sheena (part border collie/part balloon) and 33 sheep (Shetland/Cheviot crossbreeds by the looks of them).

Getting there: Wait for the ferry to dock at Lerwick before wiping away the vomit stains and peeling joyfully away up the A970. Bob up and down for 33 miles (one for each sheep), following the signs to Hillswick. Slide right up the B9078 and 2½ miles later you'll come to an unmarked left turn to an unmarked farmhouse guarded by an unmarked border collie/balloon. It will be raining. Welcome to Zoar, Britain's most northerly zed. Worth the journey.

What's there?: A 1950s crofter's house; the ruins of a much older crofter's house; the ruins of another crofter's house which is older than the current one but not as old as the other one; some grass; some cliffs; 33 sheep.

Fig. 2.

Things to do: Watch the rain. Brave the rain to gather peats. Return to farmhouse to ask what peats look like. Go back outside. Identify peats. Bring one in. Hide it in the corner just in case it's not actually a peat. Give up gathering peats. Start counting sheep. Drift off to sleep. Wake up. Watch the rain.

THINGS TO LOOK OUT FOR

☞ *The Heads of Grocken over which, a century ago, a doomed collector of gulls' eggs fell, followed in the 1960s by a horse called Bob* (fig. 3) – 1 POINT; 2 POINTS if you are called Bob, or you feel that you yourself are doomed in

Fig. 3.

some way you can't quite put your finger on.

Fig. 4.

Fig. 5.

Main gate (fig. 4) – 1 POINT. That's it. It's just a gate.

The notorious Bath of Zoar (fig. 5) – 3 POINTS; 5 POINTS if it was the sight of the bath that first made you feel doomed in some way you couldn't quite put your finger on. ☜

Nearest pub: Mid Brae Inn (fig. 2), Brae (thirteen miles), though the Hillswick village hall (two miles) has a bar of sorts every Wednesday from 8.30 p.m. Bring your own atmosphere.

Nearest public phone box: Behind the Hillswick Shop (fig. 6), Hillswick (three miles).

Fig. 6.

Nearest body of water: Helga Water, scene of a great boating tragedy in the early 1960s. A nine-year-old Zoarian boy saved up his pocket money to buy a toy motor boat, only to see it sink into the lake on its maiden voyage. It moulders there still. A bit eerie really. The boy moved to Berkshire.

What's furry?: Frog orchid (flowers May to August), heath spotted orchid (flowers May to July), whimbrel (flies about), black-legged kittiwake (squawks).

What lives in the green bins?: The *Shetland Times* (every Friday), the *Shetland Weekly* (once every 168 hours), the *Shetland Post* (every second Thursday of the month), *60 North* (formerly *Shetland Seafood News*), mammoths.

Role in Civil War: Only slight, being over 200 miles north-east of Carbisdale, the nearest battle. This didn't stop Queen Henrietta Maria from blithely offering the Shetlands to Sweden in return for support for her husband Charles. The Swedes politely declined and Zoar remained Scottish. Not that the islanders knew much about their would-be change of nationality — information travelled so slowly in those days that news of the Civil War failed to reach them until 1922, which was unfortunate because at the time many were still reeling from the shock of the death of Edward I.

Claim to fame: If the sheep at Zoar formed a football team, its fans could indulge in the chant: 'One zed in Scotland, there's only one zed in Scotland', though they might choose not to do so.

Killer fact: Every day, 3,000 people in the Shetland islands think about suicide.

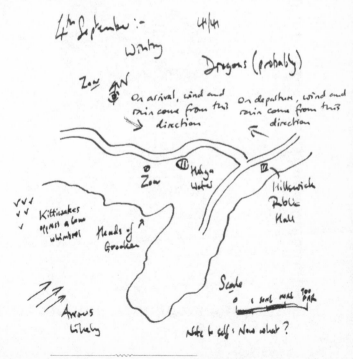

34
Zone Point

Our Ships Are Sealed

Picturesqueness	$^6/_6$
Acuity	$^5/_6$
Slant	$^6/_6$

Why's it called that?: This last gasp of the Roseland Peninsula (fig. 1) appears in the 1939 *Penguin Guide to Cornwall*

Fig. 1.

as Zoze Point. This was presumably a cunning ploy to fool potential invading forces, many of whom would have purchased the first edition guide as a necessary preamble to the conquest of the British Isles. In case this didn't work, as a Plan B the government cannily installed an anti-aircraft gun there as well. These two measures combined to keep the area free from unwelcome intrusion for the following six years.

Careless chalk may cost lives, but it's probably safe now to reveal that Zone Point derives its name from the Cornish 'penn saven' or 'point of the cleft'. Write this down. Learn it. Destroy the evidence.

Where is it?: Home to a Man whose name is Asset but

Fig. 2.

whose surname, Liability, is revealed only when the mournful yapping of the Dogs of War is heard on the Ill Winds of Change That Blow Nobody Good.

Where exactly?: OS Landranger Map 204: SW8430 (fig. 2).

No, where *exactly*?: In the sea but not of it.

Population: 0.

Getting there: For a pleasant jaunt along the front, alight at Falmouth Docks station rather than Falmouth Town. From June to October you may take the ferry to St Mawes from Customs House Quay. The rest of the year you'll have to head further north to the Prince of Wales Pier. At St Mawes, check whether it's Easter to October. If so, board the tiny ferry for Place. If not, take the A3078 through St Just in Roseland and, at Trewithian, careen right and head through Gerrans and Froe, turning left along the Military Road to St Anthony Head. Zone Point is a short stroll south through the former battery and along the coast. If it *is* Easter to October, you will have landed safely in Place, a part of Cornwall so beautiful as to leave one almost mute. Pass the cottage where H.V. Morton spent an evening in 1926 listening to music from a London club on the wireless and turn right for St Anthony Head. Zone Point is a short stroll south through the former battery and along the coast, just like in winter.

Fig. 3.

What's there?: The usual coastal paraphernalia — cliffs, rocks, beach, sea, gun emplacement.

Things to do: Stare at the horizon. The sea and the sky may appear to meet there but the reality is wildly at odds with your perception of it, as you would find out if you only took the trouble to go there to see for yourself.

THINGS TO LOOK OUT FOR

☞ *A flight of stairs, beautiful yet tragic* (fig. 4) — 2 POINTS.

A platform for the machinery of war, a solid basis for the building blocks of peace. Discuss (fig. 3) — 2 POINTS.

Rocks, pithy yet playful (fig. 5) — 1 POINT. ☜

Nearest pub: By land, the Royal Standard in Gerrans. However, the numerous hostelries across the Percuil River in St Mawes are closer and can be

Fig. 4.

reached directly from Zone Point by grey seal, although you may have to build up some rapport with the creatures before attempting this.

Fig. 5.

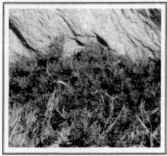

Fig. 6.

Nearest public phone box: By land, Gerrans. By river, St Mawes — usual terms and conditions apply.

Nearest body of water: Usually the sea, sometimes the tears of grey seals.

What's furry?: The stiff-winged fulmar, the ignoble shag, the common scurvy-grass (fig. 6).

What lives in the green bins?: Gorse, batteries.

Role in Civil War: An unparalleled vantage point from which to view the three Parliamentary ships that foundered in a storm and were forced into Falmouth harbour. Since the town was a Cavalier stronghold at the time, they judiciously declared for the King, a man they'd always considered a lovely bloke who was just a bit misunderstood.

Claim to fame: Saw its finest hour in World War II, of course, when its gun emplacement helped to protect the major naval port of Falmouth.

Killer fact: Lovers of Cornish heathland will find a very rare tranche of it here, though to be honest it looks no different to any other swathe of gorse-choked coastland. Zone Point was also once home to a coastguard signal station that was later converted into three holiday cottages. It was eventually demolished on the grounds that it had got a bit rusty and, more to the point, was ugly beyond endurance. Subsequently bulldozed into the gun emplacement. No flowers.

Weather: Indistinct
28th April

Zone
Point

Scale

NY London Paris Münich

35

Zoons Court

"TO US"

Picturesqueness	$^2/_6$
Acuity	$^0/_6$
Slant	$^2/_6$

Why's it called that?: Sadly, unlikely to be derived from 'zoonosis' (any disease that can be transmitted from animals to humans) or 'zounds' (expression of surprise or indignation c. 1600). The possible German origin 'zu uns'

Fig. 1.

can only lead the idle and feckless into idle and feckless speculation as to why any putative German settlers would want to name the place 'to us'.

Where is it?: In Gloucestershire, in between Cheltenham and Gloucester, and not a hundred miles from the abbey that is spelt Prinknash but pronounced 'Prinnidge'.

Where exactly?: OS Landranger Map 162: SO8718 (fig. 1).

No, where *exactly*?: Girdled around by the A40, M5 and A417, Zoons Court sits like an artlessly cut gem in a setting of barbed wire.

Population: 9.

Getting there: Be warned — do not attempt to find Zoons Court under any but the most extreme of circumstances. Only when you are sure that such circumstances exist, slide north-west up the A430 from Gloucester station, right along the B4063 making sure to keep right until reaching the safe haven of a roundabout. Plough straight over (especially if driving a plough) both this one and the next. Shimmy up the Hucclecote Road and hang a left up Larkhay Road towards the church. At the end, enjoy a chicane left and then suddenly right up another Larkhay Road. Carry on for a bit before turning left into a further Larkhay Road. Take the next fork right. This private road leads to a bridge over the A417 and up to Zoons Court. It really is that simple.

What's there?: A 300-year-old house, two cottages, a

Fig. 2.

coach house, sundry farm buildings, some electricity pylons, a footpath, a windsock, an arable farm (mainly wheat, rape and barley, in case you're thinking of lunching there).

Things to do: Walk on the footpath (fig. 2). Consider the direction of the wind. Watch the collapse of Gloucester Cathedral (collapse should be arranged in advance with verger).

THINGS TO LOOK OUT FOR

Fig. 3.

☞ *The windsock* (fig. 3) — 2 POINTS; 4 POINTS if the wind foot is clearly visible.

The shot to bits man (fig. 4) — 3 POINTS; 4 POINTS if you feel shot to bits, man.

Gloucester Cathedral (fig. 5) — 1 POINT; 2 POINTS if you can see the verger making a phone call to the police. ☜

Fig. 4.

Nearest pub: Thrillingly, The Wheatsheaf on the Gloucester ring road can actually be seen from Zoons Court.

Nearest public phone box: On Zoons Road, a road that, disarmingly, does not lead to Zoons.

Nearest body of water: Horsbere Brook skirts the western edge of Zoons Court like a Dalíesque squiggle awaiting absolution.

What's furry?: Occasional hoopoe (April to September) — identifiable by its black and white markings and distinctive Mohican, a bit like how you might imagine a zebra in flight shortly after it had freed its head from a toaster.

Fig. 5.

What lives in the green bins?: Moët et Chandon jeroboae, helicopter parts.

Role in Civil War: That bang-on Parliamentarian the Earl of Essex led his forces from London through here to relieve the siege of Gloucester on the dank morning of 6 September 1643. Later in the day he won the toss, put the Cavaliers in and cleverly used the low cloud to produce some almost unplayable reverse swing. He went on to develop a revolutionary type of delivery – the 'yorker' – so called because it was employed to such devastating effect at the siege of York.

Claim to fame: According to its helicopter-flying owner, lots of famous people have visited the big house. He is, however, unwilling to name names, which is refreshing in a way in these celebrity-drenched times but, by the same token, strangely dissatisfying.

Killer fact: Just 1¾ miles from Gloucestershire airport. This means you could fly in for afternoon tea from your home in Casablanca and still get back in time for your favourite Moroccan soaps.

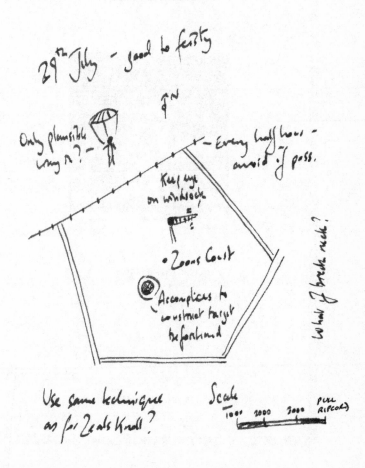

36

Zouch

Picturesqueness	$3/6$
Acuity	$4/6$
Slant	$1/6$

Why's it called that?: Perhaps the most important thing to remember when interacting with the people of Zouch is that their village rhymes not with 'mooch' or 'vouch', as might be reasonably assumed, but 'such'. As for its origins, since many of the outlying villages devoted themselves to the manufacture of arrows for Henry V's armies to dent French heads with, it is possible, if highly unlikely, that the name is derived somewhat obliquely from 'flèche'. More probable is that Zouch owes its title to the 12th-century Breton nobleman after whom nearby Ashby de la Zouch is named.

Where is it?: Encircled and harried by Derby, Nottingham, Leicester and, to a lesser extent, Barton in Fabis, Gotham and Bunny.

Where exactly?: OS Landranger Map 129: SK5023 (fig. 1).

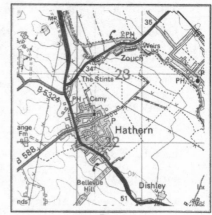

Fig. 1.

No, where *exactly*?: Where Nottinghamshire and Leicestershire meet in a grim tango to the death.

Population: About 100, depending on the day.

Getting there: The platform at Loughborough (twinned with Zamość in Poland, the Poles being great train buffs with a particular fascination for station architecture) is somewhat truncated, so any donation of breeze blocks or

Fig. 2.

cement that you might be prepared to bring along would no doubt be appreciated. Waving away the humble thanks of the locals, pour yourself out of the station, turning sharp right at the traffic lights. Take another right at the post office down Meadow Lane. Follow your nose through Stanford on Soar and Normanton on Soar and a left at the end of Moor Lane will see you safely into Zouch.

What's there?: Loads. In fact, so much that the inhabitants have to order their possess-ions alphabetically. There are boats, several bridges, a

Fig. 3.

brand new bus shelter (though like birds and nesting boxes, you may have to wait a while before you see a bus sheltering under it), some houses, a marina, a pub, a riding school, a river (fig. 2), a tow path and some weirs. Exactly the kind of village you might have wished Wilfred Owen had come from had he not been born in Oswestry.

Things to do: Learn to ride. Visit the pub. Boat. Swim. Gaze. One lifetime is not enough.

THINGS TO LOOK OUT FOR

Fig. 4.

Fig. 5.

☞ *The Footbridge of Eternal Reason* (fig. 3) — 2 POINTS.

The Weir of Seething Fury (fig. 4) — 1 POINT.

The House of Terrible Smallness (fig. 5) — 2 POINTS. ✍

Nearest pub: Unlike so many of its compatriots, Zouch has fashioned its very own pub, The Rose and Crown (fig. 6), whence boat trips along the Soar can be had at reasonable rates.

Nearest public phone box: On Main Street (yes, it's really called that), opposite the bus shelter.

Nearest body of water: The two branches of the River Soar course through the village like a catheter on horseback.

What's furry?: Guinea fowls, swans, herons, crayfish, zander and more ducks than you can shake a breadstick at.

Fig. 6.

What lives in the green bins?: The nightmares of the past, arrow heads.

Role in Civil War: This part of the Midlands was so assiduously contested during the war that there were times when you couldn't move without bumping into somebody skewering someone else over a difference of opinion regarding the governance of England. Indeed, the war itself started just up the road in Nottingham on a dank August day in 1642 when Charles I raised his standard there. Recruits for the King's army were sought from local villages such as Zouch but everyone was getting the harvest in so couldn't really be bothered. The standard blew down a week later. The writing was not so much on the wall as in the mud. Meanwhile, the chairman of a committee formed in 1644 to adjudicate between those Parliamentarians who wanted to continue fighting and those who wanted to negotiate a peace was one Zouch Tate.

Claim to fame: Zouch was probably venerable even by the time the Domesday Book recorded its existence if the recently discovered Viking remains are anything to go by. This would suggest that the village's name goes back a lot further than the 12th century and is actually a corruption of an Old Norse word such as 'geit' (goat) or 'stakkr' (rock in the sea) or even a combination of the two (apparently, if viewed from the air, the River Soar vaguely resembles a goat in the sea, in trouble).

Killer fact: Bodies float down the river from time to time from a nearby bridge.

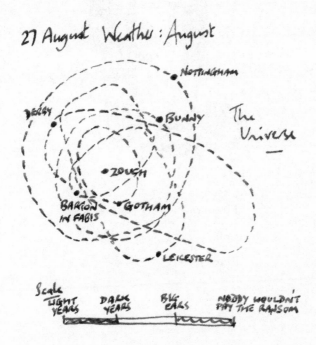

37
Zouch Farm

Picturesqueness	$3/6$
Acuity	$1/6$
Slant	$0/6$

Why's it called that?: The crest of Lord Zouch of Mortimer can be viewed in a church at nearby Stanford in the Vale, so some connection with the noble family might be assumed. Romantics still cling to the possibility that the farm derives its name from the Italian 'zucchetto', a Roman Catholic clergyman's skullcap (black for a priest, purple for a bishop, red for a cardinal, white for the Pope). However, source documents citing the harvesting of zucchetti on local farms have proved, at best, unreliable.

Where is it?: Amid an Oxfordshire countryside strewn, or perhaps riven, with electricity pylons.

Where exactly?: OS Land-ranger Map 164: SU5295 (fig. 1).

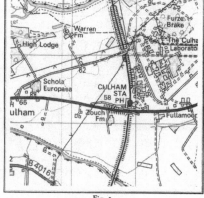

Fig. 1.

No, where *exactly*?: Very handily placed for the fusion energy research centre at Culham (take your own atoms).

Population: 3.

Getting there: One might be forgiven for thinking that Culham station, if not the entire Didcot to Oxford line, was invented specifically with Zouch Farm in mind. Forgiveness, by the way, is a Good Thing in and of itself, irrespective of the offence for which it is sought. In fact, even if it isn't sought, it remains a Good Thing and much to be wondered at. With this in mind, slip out of the station, past the pub, take a right and, when you meet the main road, go right again. Zouch Farm (fig. 2) is first on your left. The average amateur tricyclist should be able to knock off the entire journey in under a minute, depending on traffic conditions.

What's there?: A 750-acre arable farm (wheat, oilseed rape, beans), two houses, barns, converted stables, electricity pylons, contract pigs, and a Roman villa or a Roman village or similar, or at least the remains of same.

Fig. 2.

Things to do: Contract pigs. Expand them back to normal size before anyone notices. Confuse your elderly relatives by slurring your delivery of the term 'contract pigs' so that they are under the impression you're inviting them to play 'contract bridge'. How you all laughed.

Things to do in the rain: Sing. Listen to that odd fizzing sound that rain makes when it hits electricity cables. Wonder if electrically charged raindrops can kill you.

THINGS TO LOOK OUT FOR

Fig. 3.

Fig. 4.

☞ *A ball of mistletoe etched against a grey sky* (fig. 3) — 3 POINTS.

Toadstool with planter and stone (fig. 4) — 2 POINTS.

A country stile (fig. 5) — 1 POINT; 2 POINTS if you spot the country it's in. ☜

Nearest pub: The Railway Inn. It's that building by the station that appears to be brooding over something that happened to it five or six years ago. A missed opportunity, perhaps, or a slight from an acquaintance.

Nearest public phone box: The phone closest to hand crow-wise loiters in Appleford, a mile to the south. However, to reach this takes one west, south and east and, more pertinently, past a perfectly usable phone box in Culham.

The matter becomes further muddied by the fact that, twice an hour, the Appleford phone suddenly becomes the more convenient of the two again by being just a stop away on the railway. Agatha Christie would have loved it. The murderer could easily have made the phone call to the theatre in London by leaving at five and twenty past and taking the train to Appleford, thus ensuring that no one saw him use the Culham phone. Obvious really, but it took Poirot to spot it.

Fig. 5.

Nearest body of water: The River Thames, or Isis as it becomes in these parts, or even more accurately, the Clifton Cut.

What's furry?: Red kites, mainly. Apparently, these can be discerned by their V-shaped tails, as opposed to buzzards, whose tails are squarer, like toast.

What lives in the green bins?: The fall-out from the electricity passing overhead. Season tickets. Kisses.

Role in Civil War: Royalist cavalry frequently patrolled around Abingdon so would have attempted to smoke out any Parliamentarians who might be sneaking around Zouch Farm with their pikes up their sleeves. Charles I, who was no great strategist, withdrew from the town in May 1644 to make his army at Oxford 'more nimble'. This left the Roundheads to withdraw their pikes, get the blood going in their arms again, and wander into an undefended Abingdon.

Claim to fame: Zouch Farm sits blithely opposite the world's largest tokamak (if you have to ask, you shouldn't). This is operated by the Culham Science Centre on behalf of the whole of Europe. Oddly, very few Europeans ever seem to thank us for this.

Killer fact: The farm lies in a loop of the Thames just to the east of an enigma. The Swift Ditch is now a backwater of the river but for seven centuries up to about 1790 it was the main channel. Now nobody knows whether the Ditch is the true course of the Thames fallen on hard times, making the Thames at Abingdon a mere man-made cut, or vice versa. Who can sleep when such questions assail us?

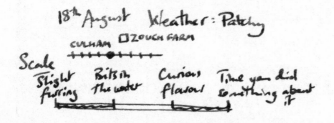

38
Zouches Farm

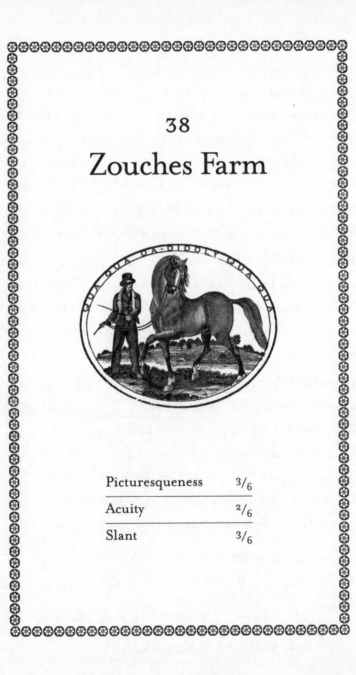

Picturesqueness	3/6
Acuity	2/6
Slant	3/6

Why's it called that?: Named after the redoubtable Joan Zouche, a 16th-century prioress famed for the resolute defence of her nunnery against brigands, footpads and the like. When Henry VIII dissolved her nunnery, she and her clutch of nuns followed him around the country like a bevy of Banquo's ghosts, except that they were still alive and Shakespeare hadn't written *Macbeth* by then, or indeed had the presence of mind to be born. Such behaviour was apt to bring about the shuffling off of

Fig. 1.

one's mortal coil pretty sharpishly in those days, so Archbishop Cranmer intervened and persuaded Henry to give Joan a pension, a house and, generously, some of the land he'd just stolen from the nunnery. In 1539, the property became Zouches Farm.

Where is it?: At two miles, the farm is not all that distant from the source of the River Lea, though probably still too far away to serve as changing rooms.

Where exactly?: OS Landranger Map 166: TL0421 (fig. 1).

No, where *exactly*?: Towering majestically over the time-worn

Icknield Way, an oasis of Chiltern green in a conurbation of Lutonian-Dunstablian brown, albeit a brown with some small bits of green in it.

Population: 9.

Getting there: Forging a path to Zouches Farm is initially as hard and unforgiving as a frozen Brussels sprout but then suddenly becomes as easy as pap, as if you'd kept the gelid brassica for long enough in your mouth for it to melt into a green slush. Swallow hard and leave Luton station by

Fig. 2.

the transparent lift, taking advantage of the generous vistas afforded of the service road, and head left. At the end, take a right under the bridge, a left at the roundabout, first right, left at the roundabout then right up Park West Street. Follow this round, over a traffic light, and turn left at the end. You are still in Luton. However, the road you are now on will eventually deposit you at Zouches Farm. Just go under the bridge, up the hill, past the country park, under the MI, through Caddington, and the farm (fig. 2) is on the right where the road bends left.

What's there?: 340 acres of arable farm, two houses, a well, some sheds, a one-eyed horse, a pond, some public footpaths and a telecommunications mast bristling with things our grandparents couldn't possibly have envisaged in their wildest dreams in the sleepy bucolic bliss that was their childhood.

Things to do: Avoid the gaze of the one-eyed horse. Bristle.

THINGS TO LOOK OUT FOR

☞ *Gate in a warm winter jacket* (fig. 3) – 1 POINT.

Blank signboard (fig. 4) – 1 POINT (if you have also spotted the blank signboard of Zeals Knoll, consider yourself to have collected the set).

Fig. 3.

Folly cunningly disguised as a telecommunications mast to blend in with the landscape of modern Britain (fig. 5) – 2 POINTS. ☜

Fig. 4.

Nearest pub: Crows unerringly fly to The Highwayman at Dunstable but walkers find it swifter to hack across the fields to The Chequers at Caddington.

Fig. 5.

Nearest public phone box: On the green at Caddington, a place that shivers at night.

Nearest body of water: A pond near the farmhouse catches water. What do *you* do?

What's furry?: Nightjars, skylarks, all three common woodpeckers — indeed almost any bird whose name is composed of two nouns.

What lives in the green bins?: Bucolics Anonymous flyers; one very large eye.

Role in Civil War: The Parliamentarians were mustard keen on the farm and visited often, most significantly in the days after the battle of Edgehill when Essex pounded through here on his way to defend London.

Claim to fame: Farmer John Zouche, the last of the Zouches of Zouches Farm, supplemented his income with some nocturnal highwaymanery. He owned two identical horses whom no one had seen together, so everyone assumed he had just the one. Remember this because it's important later on. Always working alone, Zouche's modus operandi was to sneak alongside pack trains lumbering up Watling Street and covertly lead off a horse, baggage and all, into the darkness. One night his luck ran out and he found himself being chased by some law-enforcement types. He high-tailed it home, pushed his horse into a well, and got into bed. When the rozzers arrived, he pretended to have been asleep. Unconvinced, they strode to his stables, threw open the door and ... found his horse, neither sweating nor lathering, and obviously unridden that night. Zouche's close shave apparently caused him to retire from his life of crime and he died peacefully in his bed. The thoughts of the dead horse are not recorded.

Fig. 6.

Killer fact: The ghost of a highwayman is said to canter around the farm (fig. 6) at night, though there is some dispute as to whether the apparition is that of John Zouche or local boy Dick Turpin, since the ghost wears a mask, like it would. More disturbingly, the crying of a phantom baby is said to have been heard in the farmhouse.

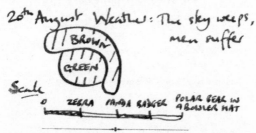

20th August Weather: The sky weeps, men suffer

BROWN
GREEN

Scale
0   ZEBRA   PANDA BADGER   POLAR BEAR IN A BOWLER HAT

39

Zulu Bank

Picturesqueness	$5/6$
Acuity	$4/6$
Slant	$0/6$

Why's it called that?: Not, as widely believed, a corruption of 'Tallulah Bankhead', although it is true to say that the triangular stretch of sand off the north Devon coast does resemble to some degree the hairstyle she favoured for her role in *Lifeboat*, Alfred Hitchcock's 'gosh that's torn it, we've been torpedoed and we're bobbing about on the waves with the U-boat captain who nailed us' hard stare-fest.

Where is it?: Under water, then not.

Where exactly?: OS Landranger Map 180: SS4332 (fig. 1).

No, where *exactly*?: At the very mouths of the rivers Taw and Torridge and growing larger every year because no one can be bothered to dredge the channel any more.

Population: None, though cockles are rumoured.

Getting there: Getting away may be a wiser option since Zulu Bank apparently boasts areas of quicksand and tides that nip in like a hare chased by whippets. Other than that, it's really quite nice. Roll out of Barnstaple station and merge seamlessly with the cycle path opposite.

Fig. 1.

This used to be a railway line that in happier days carried

merry bands of pleasure-seekers along the coast to Instow and beyond. The former station at Fremington is now a tea shop across the Taw from the RAF station which was once home to fighter pilot Flt Lt 'Bimbo' Hanson, the very mention of whose name terrified generations of schoolchildren. Smile knowingly at the waitress and continue to Instow where, in the summer months, a gentleman fresh from a dream about frozen carrots which he cannot understand will bear you over to Appledore. In non-summer months, you will be obliged to ferry yourself

Fig. 2.

over or traverse the Torridge by means of the hideous A39 or the considerably more pleasing Bideford/East-the-Water crossing and double back to Appledore. However arrived, follow the coast road through and out the other side. Take the first right and forge on to Northam Burrows Country Park, a haven disfigured by a golf course but adorned by wild horses (fig. 2). At the end of the road, abandon your pedalling activities and trudge north-west into the wind. Zulu Bank is the vast stretch of sand accessible over a scattering of rocks. Unless, of course, you have misjudged your arrival, in which case Zulu Bank is out there somewhere under the waves. Disappointing, really, but it goes to prove the value of forward planning.

What's there?: Sand.

Things to do: Study the sand. After a while, look up at the surging tide. Run through usual stages of shock, anger, denial and resignation. Wave arms about. See life flash before eyes, including the incident with the trident. Feel grip of lifeboatman's hands on your shoulders. Wish you hadn't made such a fool of yourself. Vow to change your life from that moment on. Return home.

Things to do two weeks later: Laugh it off as an amusing episode. Carry on as if it hadn't happened. Learn nothing.

THINGS TO LOOK OUT FOR

Fig. 3.

☞ *Tide in* (fig. 3) — 1 POINT (largely consolatory).

Tide out (fig. 4) — 1 POINT.

Ken (fig. 5) — 2 POINTS. ☜

Nearest pub: The Royal George at Appledore. Sea views.

Nearest public phone box: Next to the Beaver Inn, which is next to the Royal George. Sea views.

Fig. 4.

Fig. 5.

Nearest body of water: At low tide: the sea. At high tide: itself.

What's furry?: Are cockles furry? Probably not. In which case, you may have to make do with a variety of gulls wheeling above, while down below stalk waders such as the affable dunlin and the swoony avocet.

What lives in the green bins?: Flotsam, jetsam. The sea is the ultimate recycler. Or death is. One or the other anyway.

Role in Civil War: Witnessed much to-ing and fro-ing and generalised biffing. The Royalists besieged and accepted the surrender of the Roundhead fort at Appledore in 1643. Prince Charles popped in for a visit two years later and apparently had some coins minted there, which is a nice trick if you can carry it off. Cromwell was not to be denied, however, and he re-took Appledore, Zulu Bank and all, on 20 April 1646. Handshakes all round.

Claim to fame: The Vikings splashed about here in 878 and fought a big battle with some Saxons led by Odda, Duke of Devon. Odder still, the Nordic raiders came off worse. One hundred and ninety-one years later, King Harold's three illegitimate sons crossed the bank with around 50 ships but got rather beaten up by the Normans, much in the same way that their father had done.

Killer fact: Zulu Bank is tacitly referred to in Charles Kingsley's *Westward Ho!*, a book that gave its name to the dispiriting apology for a human settlement just along the coast. Mrs Leigh looks out over the sands to see her son returning in his ship. You'll have to read the rest of the book yourself. I'm not sure, but I think there's a lot of shouting in it.

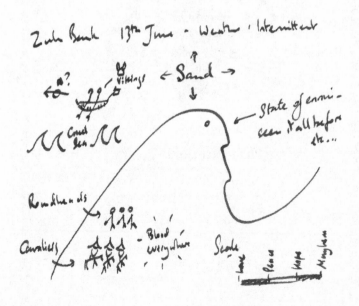

40
Zulu Buildings

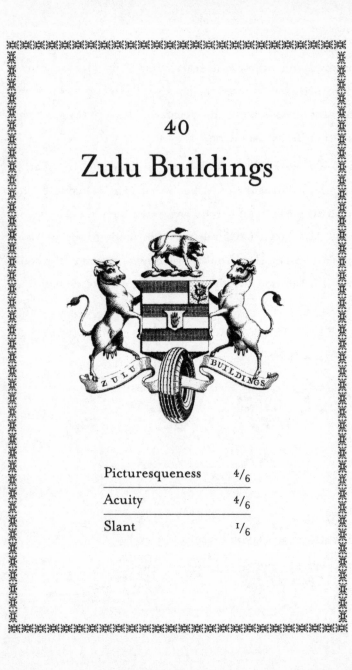

Picturesqueness	4/6
Acuity	4/6
Slant	1/6

Why's it called that?: Ho hum, it's not called that any more. It now goes by the name of Zulu Farm which puts it in direct competition with the other Zulu Farm which, needless to say, is no longer a farm. The Zulu half of the name stems from the fact that the farm was bought by a colonel returning from the Zulu Wars in 1879. The Buildings half refers to the buildings.

Where is it?: In the White Horse Vale — known officially as Vale of White Horse, the sort of name you might expect to come from someone whose English is very good but which lets them down on the odd occasion.

Where exactly?: OS Landranger Map 174: SU2586 (fig. 1).

No, where *exactly*?: On the B4000. If you have to have roads at all, they might as well have names like this.

Population: 10.

Getting there: Set off brightly from the Wiltshire town of Swindon. Try not to be upset by the size of Swindon — it got that big when it knew no better and now it's a bit late to do anything about it. Take a left out of the station, straight on at the next two roundabouts,

Fig. 1.

right at the next, then first left onto a road that suddenly goes out of control towards the end before depositing you at yet another roundabout. Carve a route more or less straight over onto the B4006, across the next roundabout and left at the following one. At the end, turn right. This road should lead you up over the A419(T) and out of Swindon. If instead you find yourself on an industrial estate or grappling with a non-coniferous forest, try starting again. If, by some happy chance, you do find yourself soaring high above the A419 on your way south-east into Oxfordshire, feel free to continue in like manner to Lower Wanborough. There take a left through Hinton Parva, Bishopstone, Idstone and Ashbury, where a further left onto the B4000 will see you reach Zulu Buildings before nightfall.

Fig. 2.

What's there?: Two hundred acres, a brace of cottages, 160 dairy cows (fig. 2), some barns and sheds, a footpath to Bourton, some hay (fig. 6), numerous tyres, and six cats: Molly, Dolly, Amber, Josie, Ruby and 'a feral cat with no name' whom, for neatness' sake, we shall call Dave. The whole kit and caboodle is owned by the Church of England.

Things to do: Milk cows. Wait for the cows to come home. Seek ordination.

THINGS TO LOOK OUT FOR

Fig. 3.

☞ *Amber, looking a mite restive* (**fig. 3**) — 2 POINTS.

Ancient Egyptian long-eared inscrutable mammalian creature (**fig. 4**) — 2 POINTS.

Tyres (don't buy the farmer's car — it must get through a set a week) (**fig. 5**) — 1 POINT. ☜

Fig. 4.

Nearest pub: The Rose and Crown, Ashbury — the one remaining pub in Oxfordshire that offers to tumble-dry the clothes of drinkers caught out by inclement weather.

Nearest public phone box: Reputed to be in the very centre of Idstone.

From the farm, the phone box can be reached via a pleasantly pastoral footpath, thus giving you something to relate when you arrive.

Fig. 5.

Fig. 6.

Nearest body of water: A stream flows through the gardens of the farm's houses on its way to the mighty Thames.

What's furry?: The usual assortment of foxes, badgers, bunnies and deer. Usual, that is, if you live in the English countryside. If such a combination were discovered living in the Qattara Depression, say, or the Marianas Trench, it would cause quite a stir.

What lives off the green bins?: Dave the cat.

Role in Civil War: On 18 September 1643, the Earl of Essex was marching his army towards London when he was intercepted by Prince Rupert at Aldbourne Chase, just seven miles to the south of the farm. A few years later, Zulu Buildings' near neighbour, Ashdown House, was built for

Charles I's sister, Elizabeth, Queen of Bohemia, but she had the bad manners to die before it was finished.

Claim to fame: White Horse Vale was immortalised — if indeed a non-living thing can be said to be given the gift of eternal life without the giver at any point actually bringing the thing itself to life in order to enjoy its eternal state — by Thomas Hughes' seminal flayed-in-front-of-a-roasting-fire-with-an-apple-in-my-mouth-and-I-was-one-of-the-lucky-ones alma mater novel *Tom Brown's Schooldays*. Hughes himself lived in Uffington, a mere conker's flight from Zulu Buildings.

Killer fact: The Zulu War was single-handedly started by Sir Bartle Frere, a British pro-consul. Unbeknown to the British government, Frere issued King Cetshwayo with an ultimatum that included the disbanding of the Zulu army, knowing full well that this would inevitably lead to war. Thousands died on both sides before Cetshwayo was captured and Zululand annexed. Between ourselves, with the monstrously incompetent and duplicitous Lord Chelmsford leading the British army, it's a surprise that anyone got back from Zululand to buy farms in Oxfordshire, let alone celebrate their part in the war.

17th August   Weather: Kempt

Why Italy? With whom?

41
Zulu Farm

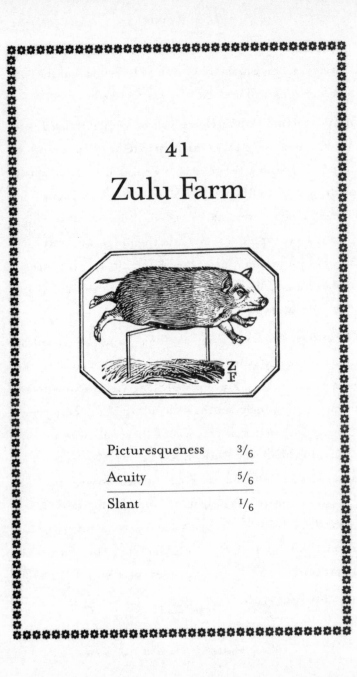

Picturesqueness	$3/6$
Acuity	$5/6$
Slant	$1/6$

Fig. 1.

Why's it called that?: Don't be fooled by the nouveau-naive sign: Zulu Farm (fig. 1) is no longer a farm. The owners presumably felt they couldn't just write the word 'Zulu' in case passers-by who knew a member of the Bantu people dropped by on the off chance that the sign might refer to their friend. The owners of the farm — originally called Zulu Barn — chose the name to commemorate the Zulu Wars. Very fond of the Empire, we were.

Where is it?: Not so much caught between a rock and a hard place as between a power station and an atomic research centre. Assuming that atomic research is quite hard, one must assume that the power station is the rock. Of course, if we could derive power from rocks, we prob-

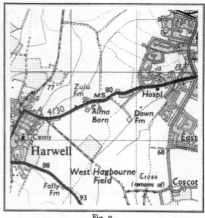

Fig. 2.

ably wouldn't be so keen on atomic research.

Where exactly?: OS Landranger Map 174: SU5089 (fig. 2).

No, where *exactly*?: Not so much caught between a rock and a hard place as between Didcot and Harwell. Assuming that Didcot is not the home of rock etc. etc.

Population: 6.

Getting there: Alight at Didcot station where you'd be best advised to swing right, take the first left, hurtle right to the end, hang a right, and forge straight over the roundabout onto the B4493. Before you know it you'll be speeding out of Didcot and into the arms of Zulu Farm.

What's there?: Two houses, a grain store, a yard, an engineering works.

Fig. 3.

Things to do: Store grain. Manufacture sundry accessories for farms (fig. 6). The most popular products to leave the strictly metaphorical gates of Zulu Farm are huts for free-ranging outdoorsy pigs, hurdles and strictly literal gates. Understandably, given the jobs dependent on the works, the pubs of south Oxfordshire do not throb to the debate about whether it is cruel to make pigs race over hurdles. Local wisdom dictates that our porcine friends enjoy it, 'otherwise they wouldn't do it, would they?'

THINGS TO LOOK OUT FOR

☞ *Pig huts: roughly modelled on the WWII Anderson Shelter. If Oxfordshire is carpet-bombed in the near future, only the pigs will survive* (fig. 4) — 3 POINTS.

Grain store, presumably holds more than one (fig. 3) —1 POINT.

Didcot Power Station: rising out of the fields like the deformed hand of a buried cement giant, it satisfies the electrical power needs of all Didcot (fig. 5) — 2 POINTS. ✌

Fig. 4.

Fig. 5.

Nearest pub: The Crispin, half a mile away at Harwell. If full or carpet-bombed, there's always the White Hart next door. However, if you have one of those allergies that prevents you from entering any drinking establishment whose name does not include the phrase 'load of mischief', you'll have to trek four miles south-east to The Load of Mischief at Blewbury.

Nearest public phone box: In 1715, the year the Jacobite rebellion was suppressed in Britain, Louis XV began his 60-year hold on power in France, and Frances Geering gave some rather tasteful almshouses to the poor of Harwell. The telephone box is opposite them. This is just as well because it's a tricky business siting a phone box opposite a suppression or a reign. History, as ever, emphasises the so-called major events at the expense of the really important ones. Demand something better.

Nearest body of water: A stream fed by a spring at the bottom of the field. There's a certain beauty in the imprecision of it.

What's furry?: Reeve's muntjac, the smallest deer in Britain — it's about the size of a labrador. If you can't imagine a labrador, think of a badger so large that it could eat a lava lamp in about half a dozen bites. The muntjacs were brought to Woburn from south-east China in 1838 and some of the more enterprising individuals escaped. Their descendants have lived in the wild ever since, some making it to Zulu Farm. The British population of muntjacs is roughly 40,000 and is increasing by about 10% per year, so you might be advised to bring your lava lamps in from the garden at night.

What lives in the green bins?: Lava, oil, wires, plugs, broken glass.

Role in Civil War: During the conflict Charles I is known to have slept at the manor house in Childrey, a village nine miles to the west. Doubtless his daily constitutional included a good hike east each morning.

Claim to fame: Zulu Farm is probably best known as a handy jumping-off point for Harwell's atomic research station. As such, it forms a pleasing counter-balance to Zouch Farm (37) and its fusion energy research centre. Curiously, the people bent on pulling tiny things apart are only a handful of miles from the people sticking tiny things together. Sometimes one can have too much irony.

Fig. 6.

Killer fact: In some ghastly incidence of lightning striking twice in the same place while in reality striking in two places separated by over 130 miles, Zulu Farm's proximity to the A34(T) is mirrored by Zeaston's A38(T) trauma.

18ᵗʰ August Weather: Corrupted
Does she know any Italians?

VISITING RECORD

	DATE VISITED	POINTS ACCRUED	WEATHER	SOUNDS	NOTES
1 Zabulon					
2 Zacry's Islands					
3 Zantman's Rock					
4 Zawn a Bal					
5 Zawn Kellys					
6 Zawn Organ					
7 Zawn Reeth					
8 Zeal					
9 Zeal Farm (NW Devon)					
10 Zeal Farm (NE Devon)					
11 Zeal Farm (SE Devon)					
12 Zeal Farm (Somerset)					
13 Zeal Monachorum					
14 Zeals					
15 Zeals House					
16 Zeals Knoll					
17 Zeaston					
18 Zelah					
19 Zelah Farm					
20 Zelah Hill					
21 Zell House Farm					

	DATE VISITED	POINTS ACCRUED	WEATHER	SOUNDS	NOTES
22 Zempson					
23 Zennor					
24 Zennor Head					
25 Zennor Quoit					
26 Zig Zag Hill					
27 Zion Hill Farm (Hants)					
28 Zion Hill Farm (Yorks)					
29 Zion Place					
30 Zion's Hill					
31 Zoar (Cornwall)					
32 Zoar (Devon)					
33 Zoar (Shetland)					
34 Zone Point					
35 Zoons Court					
36 Zouch					
37 Zouch Farm					
38 Zouches Farm					
39 Zulu Bank					
40 Zulu Buildings					
41 Zulu Farm					

BIBLIOGRAPHY

1000 Cornish Place Names Explained, Julyan Holmes; Truran Books, 2004

Alpha Beta, John Mann; Headline, 2000

The Alphabet, David Sacks; Hutchinson, 2003

The Alphabet Abecedarium, Richard A. Firmage; Bloomsbury, 2000

Battles Royal, H. Miles Brown; Libra Books 1982

Civil War, Trevor Royal; Little, Brown, 2004

Dean Prior, Rev. C.J. Perry Keane; William Brendon and Sons, 1930?

Dunsford and Doddiscombsleigh Parish Magazine, various authors;
  Dunsford and Doddiscombsleigh Parish, 2003

Legacies, Vic Lea; The Book Castle, no date

The Parish Church of Saint Peter the Apostle, Zeal Monachorum, Devon,
  Rev. J.W.G. Godeck; J.W.G. Godeck, 1991

Penguin Guides – Cornwall, J.W. Lambert; Penguin, 1939

Penguin Guides – Berks and Oxon, R.L.P. Jowitt; Penguin, 1950

A Tale of Two Manors – Zeals, A Wiltshire Village, Gwyneth F. Jackson,
  Marguerite White et al.; Dickins Printers, 2000?

Zennor and the Wayside Folk Museum, Mike Robinson; Wayside Folk
  Museum, no date

ACKNOWLEDGEMENTS

The author wishes to thank the following for their help in the production of this guide:

Brent Clark, Andy and Rachel Thacks-Jones, Clive 'Plucky Moroccans' Wills, the Scots of Zoar (Devon), Gareth and Val, Peter and Jenny Sinnett, Diane and Noel, Bridget Knott, Rachel Kehoe, Emma Johnson, James and Carol, Wendy Edgar, Geoff and Hazel Wills, Bethnal Green and Barbican Libraries, Katy the Kick Boxer, Gill Nicholson, Stephen Pugsley, Damian 'Two Hats' and Renu Basher, Kevin Pender, Jeremy Phillips, Terry Hiron, Richard Larn, Hugh Town Sophie, Janne Field, Brian and Sarah Harris, Charlotte and Anne Jackson, Magda Robson, Meryl Tovey, the Kernows, James Cherry and Amanda Dickson, Ray Hayles, the Zennor Wayside Museum, Hannah Monkhouse and Peter Edwards, best English teacher a boy could have.

><><